Hertfordshire

Edited by Steve Twelvetree

YoungWriters
First published in Great Britain in 2004 by:
Young Writers
Remus House
Coltsfoot Drive
Peterborough
PE2 9JX
Telephone: 01733 890066
Website: www.youngwriters.co.uk

SB ISBN 1 84460 511 6

Foreword

Young Writers was established in 1991 and has been passionately devoted to the promotion of reading and writing in children and young adults ever since. The quest continues today. Young Writers remains as committed to engendering the fostering of burgeoning poetic and literary talent as ever.

This year's Young Writers competition has proven as vibrant and dynamic as ever and we are delighted to present a showcase of the best poetry from across the UK. Each poem has been carefully selected from a wealth of *Once Upon A Rhyme* entries before ultimately being published in this, our twelfth primary school poetry series.

Once again, we have been supremely impressed by the overall high quality of the entries we have received. The imagination, energy and creativity which has gone into each young writer's entry made choosing the best poems a challenging and often difficult but ultimately hugely rewarding task - the general high standard of the work submitted amply vindicating this opportunity to bring their poetry to a larger appreciative audience.

We sincerely hope you are pleased with our final selection and that you will enjoy *Once Upon A Rhyme Hertfordshire* for many years to come.

Contents

Trent CE Primary School

The Poems

The Shadow

He's always behind me,
In front and beside me,
You see him in sunlight,
But not in rain,
He walks around with me
And sees everything I see,
Walking only in sunshine
And feeling no pain.

He's black and he's streamline,
An imprinted 'me' sign,
He's a copycat too
And jumps on the wall,
He never says anything,
He's even owned by a king,
He always wants to join in,
He's never not there to call.

Lizzie Minnis (10)
Bovingdon Primary School

The Story Of Lizzie Lionheart

She stands, she stares, she looks nowhere
This is the girl who lives in care
No mum, no dad, well no one yet
She always forgets to put her alarm clock on set
She looks to the right and then to the other
She doesn't even know if she has a mother
She is confused about her part
So this is the story of Lizzie Lionheart.

Natalie Reid (10)
Bovingdon Primary School

Miss 007

There's this lady down our street
Called Miss 007,
No one knows who she is,
This mystery from Heaven.

She's as sly as a fox,
As quiet as a mouse,
She travels the world,
From house to house.

It's said her life
Is full of leisure,
People say her house
Is full of treasure.

So many questions,
We have to ask,
We long to know
About her busy task.

Rachel Horspool (9)
Bovingdon Primary School

The Dark

There's something there, there in the dark,
Is it a ghost or a man-eating shark?
Is it a monster, a witch or an elf?
Oh goodness me, I'm frightening myself!

It happens to me every night,
The minute my mum turns off the light,
An icy chill runs down my back,
I think it's courage I really lack!

The sun is rising now at last,
I'm so glad it's going so fast,
Well, now I realise, so you see,
The only scary thing is *me!*

Catherine Horspool (9)
Bovingdon Primary School

Zak Collects

Zak collects . . .
Pencils and rulers,
Hamster food
And very cool jewels,
Pens and paper,
Birds from nests,
Bits of tests,
With a disgusting vapour.

Zak collects . . .
Stones and bricks,
Golden coin money,
With honey and sticks,
Ripped up tissue,
Hats, cards and scissors,
With animals such as
Insects and lizards.

Zak Farrell (9)
Boxmoor Primary School

Autumn

Autumn is now here
Swallows fly away
The leaves are all crisp
The fog spirals in a wisp

The conkers shine beige and brown
Their cases scattered on the ground
The hedgehogs burrow in the leaves
The squirrels hide their nuts in trees.

Hayleigh Hobbs (11)
Boxmoor Primary School

I Heard A Spider Singing

I heard a spider singing,
Climbing up the wall.
He got so carried away,
He began to fall.

The voice made me shiver,
As I sat beneath the tree.
He climbed off the ball
And scuttled over to me.

He glared at me,
So I went to get a box,
Then scooped him up,
I looked in the box and there a spider was as hairy as a fox.

He had a cheesy grin,
As if he would escape,
He turned around and around,
Showing his teeth as shiny as sticky tape.

Ella McKenzie (8)
Boxmoor Primary School

Camelot Under 8s

We are Camelot under 8s
We are great
We play together
Whatever the weather
Always together
As friends forever.

Kieran Cavanagh (8)
Boxmoor Primary School

Bad Days

He got up out of bed,
As he did, he banged his head,
He stumbled down and down the stairs,
The bottom seemed to have some bears.

After he had breakfast, he felt fine,
Then he felt divine
And then he went swimming,
Then he came home, as he saw the light was dimming.

The sun was getting deeper in the sky,
When suddenly the sun went with a blink of an eye,
It was now night,
There was no lights, except the stars shining bright.

The man came home, exhausted and hungry
And lay on the sofa and played with his toy monkey,
Then he went and cooked some dinner,
But the doorbell rang and it was a singer.

He ate his supper of chips and chicken,
Then went to bed and read his book by Charles Dickens,
He felt tired and so he fell into a deep sleep
And his toy monkey tried not to make a peep!

Gemma Annis (10)
Boxmoor Primary School

The Tiger

'Get out my way,' the tiger said,
'They're going to have our head.'
'Slow down, slow down,' the lion said
'It's such a beautiful day to stay, so stay.'
'They're going to kill us,' the tiger said.
'Don't worry, they won't see us.'

Samantha Sydney (11)
Boxmoor Primary School

Nonsense Land

Once upon a time in a land near away,
Lived a nasty old prince made of clay.
Nearby in a forest was a fair witch,
Who lived in a tower with Lilo and Stitch.
Somewhere about in a very sticky bog,
Lived a green-scaled princess who had a pet log.
High in a castle by a field of rice,
Sat a dragon in a frilly dress sucking on ice.
The prince kidnapped the witch,
Who fell in love with the dragon,
Who went to slay the princess,
Who wanted to tag along.
The princess ate the dragon,
The princess ate the witch,
The princess ate the prince,
She ate Lilo and Stitch,
Snick snat
And that was the end of that!

Hannah McKenzie (11)
Boxmoor Primary School

The Beaver

The unhurried beaver,
In water a good weaver,
In catching fish a great achiever.

Sam Beasley (11)
Boxmoor Primary School

A Lost Soul

Looking for a lost soul
On his trek he needs to go
On his way he finds a hole
As he goes he takes a bow

Through a field he takes a short cut
On the route he finds a hole
He goes in and the door slides shut
Inside, ran a mouse

He goes up the creaky stairs
And into a dark room
In the room it was full of hairs
And in it he found a broom

Under the broom he found his soul
Out the house he went
He walked back past the hole
In the hole there was a dent.

Ryan Murray (10)
Boxmoor Primary School

The Lion Of The Mountain Top

Roar, you hear across the mountain
Tops and the trickle of the water
Beating against the rocks, proudly he sits
Looking for his prey, then he pounces
Catch of the day, he sees you, run!
So he sits there, eating the heart of the prey away.

Helena Mansbridge (11)
Boxmoor Primary School

I Love And Miss

Where is the sun
That I love and miss?
Where are the leaves
That I love and miss?
They're laid to rest
Because autumn is best
Golden, crispy fruit
Fresh and ripe, the autumn loot

Where are the fun days out,
That I love and miss?
Where are the pool days
That I love and miss?
Gone the splashes and crashes of swimming
But now the splash and crash of raindrops
The summer has past
It's autumn
But how long will it last?
That I love and miss.

Louise Verroken-Jones (11)
Boxmoor Primary School

A Snowy Day

I looked out my window and snow was falling,
It came down quickly, it wasn't stalling,
Then I heard my mum calling.

I grabbed my hat and coat and off I went in the snow,
Out I go, off I go!
My boots are wet and I've got a frozen toe.

It was a great day
And I hope it's here tomorrow.

Natalie Carter (10)
Boxmoor Primary School

Kookalazoky

The day was new,
We were eating looloo stew,
The zamboo trees were swaying,
The kookalazok was slaying.

So we set off to the kookalazok's lair,
Where we met a bazaky seiher,
Be careful my friends, the fiend awaits,
But we continued, for our sword he hates.

We heard a crackling sound,
We went on, guess what we found?
A dragon platinum and gold,
Looking strong and bold,
So we drew our net,
What a great beast we're going to get!

Herman Greaves (10)
Boxmoor Primary School

Fear Is . . .

Fear is the creaking of stairs at midnight,
Fear is the threatening smell of smoke from a burning house,
Fear is being lost or alone on a cold dark night,
Fear is when your nerves start bursting,
Fear is when your lips grow dry from screaming,
Fear is the graveyard, the shadows of the stones are cast on you!

Fay Breed (9)
Boxmoor Primary School

The Fearsome Beast

Lying in my dark cave
I could not hear a sound
Waiting eagerly for the brave
I crouch upon the ground

Then I hear a chink of mail
I know my prey is here
I know myself, I will not fail
He is the one with fear

I see his shadow on the wall
I'm ready now to fight
Seeing me, his pride will fall
And then my jaw will bite

Fire burning
Dragon breath
His life is turning
Now for death!

Matthew Chapman (10)
Boxmoor Primary School

Autumn!

I step on the brittle leaves,
I stare up at the bare trees.
A spiky ball upon the ground,
I crack it, a conker I have found.

The leaves rustle, as I walk on,
I listen, no swallows singing their song,
My feet are heavy upon the floor,
My legs like lead, but I walk some more.

But wait - I stop, I see a thorn,
Under the leaves, a hedgehog was born,
I start to feel cold,
Winter's yet to come, for not it's best with autumn!

Rosie Payne (11)
Boxmoor Primary School

Fading Into The Darkness

Everything around me fades to dark,
The people, the flowers, the trees with their bark.
A chilling feeling fills my bones,
The sky above me takes its tones.
A bright light shines in my face,
She steps down from it, full of grace.
'Angel,' I breathe, she takes my hand,
She leads me to her floating land.
Up some stairs, light as a feather,
No gloom here, nor rainy weather.
A sharp pain fills my chest,
I want to stay, I try my best.
But I'm falling back to Earth,
I land softly on the damp, green turf.

Abigail Bryce (11)
Boxmoor Primary School

The Old Man And The Single Snowflake

A single snowflake falling down,
Like a piece of white confetti,
As it adds to the ground like a blanket on a bed,
The fire inside wraps everyone up tight,
With a mug of hot chocolate,
As soon as everyone sees the snow
They grab a sweater and a snowsuit,
Someone bundles up some snow
And aims it at a girl,
She throws one straight back,
I watch and wish I were out there too.

Amber Bartlett (10)
Boxmoor Primary School

Scary Night!

I woke up in the night,
I heard a noise, it gave me such a fright,
I ran upstairs to tell my mum,
Little did I know she was part of the fun.
There was nowhere to go,
I was all alone,
My voice had gone funny in a different tone,
I couldn't stop, I was changing, changing,
'Abi, wake up, it's school,' my mum would say,
It was just a dream, everything's now OK!
I wonder what adventure I'll have tonight,
Hopefully one that has no fright!

Abi Acors (11)
Boxmoor Primary School

One Day I Wished!

One day I wished
That I could eat a fish

The second day I wished
That my fish was on a dish

The third day I wished
That my fish on the dish was delicious

The fourth day I wished
That my fish on the dish was delicious and turned out
To be a goodnight kiss.

Lucy Hutchinson (10)
Boxmoor Primary School

Autumn Leaves!

Leaves falling to the ground,
Slowly,
They swirl, they loop,
Quickly,
Red ones fly,
While gold ones steadily blow.

The southern birds fly their best,
While the little ones take to rest,
The robin puts on his red winter vest,
Citizens dream of south and west.

Autumn's here!

Amy Mairs (11)
Boxmoor Primary School

The Revenge Of The Dragon

The revenge is sweet,
The animals are bleat in the calm world
I could hear a noise
Fire emerging with a crackling sound

The revenge is sweet
The dragon is asleep
Snoring loudly
We get out our axe
And we slay him proudly.

Robert Antonopoulos (11)
Boxmoor Primary School

Odatch

Many suns ago in the land of snow and frost,
The Odatch haunted the forest,
When I decided to kill it,
I ran with my sword that would kill it,
As I ran with my sword I saw the tree of death,
My gasp turned icy-cold, I stared for hours,
When in the darkness I saw a pair of eyes,
I took my sword in hand and charged,
Right towards my course of death,
My blade bounced back from a feckle blow,
My anger rose and watched it draw its last breath.
I sent my sword in his back,
I saw it charge, eyes full of pain,
I drew my last breath in a gasp,
As he fell with horn in my heart,
Then I fell in a pool of blood,
Staining the ice-white snow.

Tom Woffendin (11)
Boxmoor Primary School

The Jungle

I was walking in the jungle,
With the trees above my head.
When I took a sudden stumble
And fell on mossy bed.

I went across a scallywog
And saw a bright green skizzle.
It had claws like a fizgog's,
It made me start to frizzle.

I stared through a bobala bush,
I ran through the trees with a pemple,
I gave myself a final push
And ran towards the temple.

Emily Morris (10)
Boxmoor Primary School

The Fly

The fly whizzes past,
Alerting my curious eye,
Looking up so fascinated,
By his delicate wings.

Banging and banging,
Going nowhere,
So I decided,
I'll give him some freedom.

The fly buzzes away,
Out of sight,
I wonder if,
I'll see him tonight.

Georgie Ellis (9)
Boxmoor Primary School

The Fly

The timid little fly is banging on the door,
Flapping its wings then trying again once more,
I'm flying round and round,
Like a bad-tempered butterfly,
Trying to get outside before I could die.

A little girl is coming,
But now she is running,
I'm getting very worried,
I'd better flap my wings,
I think I'd better hurry,
Before I can't fly.

Pippa Hill (10)
Boxmoor Primary School

The Fly

Little fly, little fly,
Flying around in the sky,
He turns around and sees a pie,
What a big fat fly!

One day he sees a bunny,
Then he asked for some honey,
Then he turns again and again,
Then he goes to bed again!

The next day he eats the honey,
Then he turns around
And sees more honey,
Yum, yum, yummy!

Charlotte Waugh (9)
Boxmoor Primary School

Sadness Is . . .

Sadness is when people hate you
And when you do everything wrong.
Sadness is when you are left out
And the pain of being bullied.
Sadness is when your feelings get hurt
And when you hear people shouting.
Sadness is when you are distressed
And when you are heartbroken.
Sadness is when something tragic has happened
And when you feel glum.

Zoe Brook (9)
Boxmoor Primary School

The Fly

I am a fly, innocent am I,
I flicker and flutter up in the sky,
I don't sting like a bee or itch like a flea,
I am a fly, innocent am I.

People try to hurt me,
I don't do anything wrong,
I just enjoy the scenery
And play all day long.

I bang against the pane
And try and try again,
But no one seems to help me,
Oh think of me, I am just a fly, innocent am I.

Melissa Hardy (10)
Boxmoor Primary School

Fun

Fun is the brightest colour of the rainbow,
Fun is amusements at the highest point,
Fun is a roller coaster zooming at full speed,
Fun is making a jigsaw puzzle with your mum and dad,
Fun is funfairs with dodgems bashing and crashing,
Fun is having a good night's sleep with a dream on top.

Christopher Veall (9)
Boxmoor Primary School

The Fly

I flicker and flutter
From here to there,
I whistle and whine
Through the air.

My heart beats fast
With pain and fear,
For I sense that
Danger is near.

I try to flap my wings,
I struggle, push and hack,
But a silky, sticky web
Seems to force me back.

I can feel it crawl nearer,
I am determined to get free,
But my brittle body feels weary
As it hovers above me.

It started to grumble and growl,
But then it edged away,
Something must have spooked it
And saved me from being its prey.

A fluffy, furry duster,
Whisked the web away,
Luckily I escaped
Or at least for another day.

Priya Odedra (10)
Boxmoor Primary School

The Lifestyle Of A Fly

As I hum my body vibrates,
Right through, so my insides ache,
I blindly flicker back and forth,
Darting from site to site.

I thrash myself against the windowpane,
I am eager to escape,
My fragile body quivers,
Oh how I will not despair.

The temptation of fruit is sucking me in,
I dither about and move in for the kill,
I shudder at the thrill of fruit
And absorb into the juicy peach.

The moist rain pounds against me,
Bucketing down, blurring my vision and drenching my bristly hair,
I catch a glimpse of flimsy web
And lie mild, weak and dead.

Eloise Phillips (10)
Boxmoor Primary School

Wintertime

Snow is falling to the ground,
Without making a sound,
The snow is like a white blanket,
With lots of twigs and stones inside it,
There is glittery snow,
With candles that glow
And wind that'll blow,
This is the rhyme
Because it's wintertime.

Sarah Cosgrove (7)
Boxmoor Primary School

The Horse Rhyme

Once upon a time
I had a rhyme
Stuck in my head

It was about some horses
Doing some courses
Galloping off again

The owner of the horse
Was in the stable
Writing a fable

The horse came in
The stable
And tried to eat
The fable.

Catherine Chapman (7)
Boxmoor Primary School

Elephants

Elephants are very tall
Like huge birds in the sky
Elephants have big flappy ears
Playing around and rolling on the ground
Having lots of fun
Always on the move
Never have I seen purple elephants
Trunks flying high.

Emily Crawley (8)
Boxmoor Primary School

Horses

Once upon a time
I knew a rhyme
And it went like this:
I had some horses
Who did lots of courses
Round and round our field
They walked, they trotted
Cantered and galloped
They jumped over the fence, all in a herd
And on their way they raced a bird
At last I found them up a tree
Playing hide-and-seek
Clever me!
Once upon a time
I knew a rhyme.

Kristen Hindley (7)
Boxmoor Primary School

The Fly

A fly whizzes past,
Alerting my curious eye,
Banging and banging,
Just going nowhere.

I might let you out,
Just fly out of there,
The fly buzzes away,
Out of sight,
Wondering which way to go,
Left or right?

Charlotte Bower (10)
Boxmoor Primary School

Temptation

It is like a sun without heat,
It is a hand with no grasp,
A sweet smell you can't touch,
Like an eye that is blind,
You can see it,
But you can't stroke it,
But you have to.

It's a choice between persistent longing,
Or guilt prolonging.

A tree with no leaves,
Like a life with no end,
An end with no beginning,
I know I can't,
My guilt would cling on,
If I did.

It's a choice between persistent longing,
Or guilt prolonging.

Catherine Smith (9)
Boxmoor Primary School

The Fly

I sit downstairs on the chair
Then there is a fly *buzzing* by
Around my eye

Seeing it makes me *shiver*
Looking up high
I see the fly

That annoying fly
Is being so sly
Now at the end it is going to die.

Kirsty Power (10)
Boxmoor Primary School

Fear Is . . .

Fear is the shadow of your
dressing gown moving.
Fear is the movement of the trees
blowing at midnight.
Fear is when you see a shadow
moving downstairs.
Fear is when you hear shouting
downstairs.
Fear is a pitch-black graveyard.
Fear is a haunted house at night.
Fear is when you hear creaking
on the stairs.
Fear is when you see blood
on the side of a dungeon wall.
Fear is . . .

Amy-Beth Howard (9)
Boxmoor Primary School

Party

It's party time so hooray, hooray
It's a great time to play, play
All my friends are here, here
So come on everyone!

Zoë Dennis (7)
Boxmoor Primary School

The Fly

I don't like humans,
I don't think they like me,
But I know I get on their nerves,
Especially when I'm hungry.

I flap my shimmering wings,
Darting here and there,
Even though I'm nervous,
My stomach really sings.

I see a pot of juicy jam,
Maybe too much to risk,
I visualise my life coming to an end,
Just like my poor uncle Sam.

I continue my search,
As something catches my eye,
A big blueberry pie
And there I perch.

I eat and eat until I can eat no more,
Oh just think how smart I am
And think
What the humans have in store.

I start my lazy journey,
Back to my flower,
When yet again something
Or someone snatched my vision.

A little girl splashing in her pool,
In this heat,
The blazing sunlight,
I could do with getting cool.

I fight my way through the air,
Oh no! Not again,
I start to see the light at the end of the tunnel,
This really can't be fair.

My life must stop,
All hope is lost,
I can't depend on a human demon
And there I drop.

Hannah Napthine (10)
Boxmoor Primary School

Typical Little Fly!

I'm a typical little fly,
I have no friends
And I don't know why,
I'm being honest,
It's not a lie,
I'm a typical little fly.

I see another little fly,
I wish I was with her,
Flying way up high,
I'm being honest,
It's not a lie,
I'm a typical little fly.

I start to cry,
I just want to be normal,
I think I know why,
I'm being honest,
It's not a lie,
I'm a typical little fly.

Now I know why
I have no friends
And I start to cry,
It's because I'm a typical little fly,
All I do is dart around
And hover about the ground.

Claudia Woodham (10)
Boxmoor Primary School

The Fly

I don't like humans
And they don't like me,
They hate it when
I disturb their thoughts,
By buzzing around distracting them.

I awkwardly flap
Around and around,
The huge looming daisies,
Looking for food, I only
Want my little blue body
To live.

I love weird little creatures,
The way they stutter
And they fascinate me
As they investigate my food,
Trying to keep their hairy bodies safe.

They flutter and zoom,
Seeking wearily for water,
But do they realise
The dangers of the blue stuff
They need so desperately to drink?

I stalk towards the water,
Absorbing its welcoming ripples,
My wings feel heavy,
I can't fly up,
I can't feel my legs, I'm weaker . . .

The fly sank deeper,
Like the sun behind a cloud,
I dipped my gentle, welcoming hands
Down to help him
To live.

That human was not
As bad as I thought,
Are humans as horrible
As I once believed?

Sarah Kinley (9)
Boxmoor Primary School

The Fly

I lay in bed under the covers,
I realise I'm not alone,
For a little furry creature
Has been living in my home.

Looking out the window,
Begging to get out,
Making a loud buzzing noise,
Fluttering his wings about.

Wait, he has found a crack,
A hole in the window,
He has completed his challenge,
He can finally go.

Sophie Doyle (9)
Boxmoor Primary School

A Football Match

The crowd bursting out cheers
As the teams come zooming out
Onto the muddy pitch
Owen started speeding towards the goal
But was kicked in the legs by Beckham

'Free kick!' announced the ref
Owen blasted the ball at the net
Into the goalkeeper's hands
It trickled out of his hands over the line!

Owen shouted with joy, sweat streaming down his face.

Sam Wilson (8)
Boxmoor Primary School

The Fly

I'm just a common fly,
Darting to and fro,
Absentmindedly shooting around,
Not caring where I go.

But then I'm in big danger,
I dare look ahead,
If I go much further,
I may end up dead.

I've landed in a fridge,
I flew in steady and slow,
It feels as though I'm buried,
Buried beneath the snow.

My pure aching wings
And my furry sooty legs,
Cannot go much further,
When I'm trapped between two eggs.

Why is it getting colder?
Why am I shutting my eyes?
Am I getting older
Or am I about to die?

Imogen Hudson (10)
Boxmoor Primary School

Man U Win

The crowd roars with excitement as the players burst onto the pitch
Ruud van Nistelrooy was rushing down the pitch
He blasts the ball to Scholes
He sends it trickling past Seaman
Man U win!
The blazing sun making sweat flow down their faces
Man City burst off the pitch in sadness.

Max Walker (9)
Boxmoor Primary School

Rebecca's Pockets

Rebecca collects stickers and knickers
She has in her pockets mints and flints
Having a tissue is a big issue
Paperclips and felt tips too
Cards, labels, stones and bones
Rubber and things like flubber
Twigs and wigs, clips, bricks and also sticks
Sweet wrappers and zappers
Crystals and pistols, pips and tips
In Rebecca's pockets she has lots of things.

Rebecca Hall (8)
Boxmoor Primary School

Uranus Is A Shark

Uranus is a darting shark
Patrolling the ocean
Darting from side to side
Creeping along the ocean bed
For striking its prey
Zooming and twirling
Through the rough ocean tide.

Sam Izzard (9)
Boxmoor Primary School

Funny School Days

My school has a lot of people rushing about
The lunch is always boiling hot
The sun is always blazing through our window
Making us exhausted
We go into the playground
Amy falls over with a crash!
She burst into tears
Because of the leg blood bubbling out
We play with our friends
Zooming around the playground
Louise tells a joke
We all explode with laughter.

Charlotte Blair-Smith (9)
Boxmoor Primary School

A Recipe For A Werewolf

Take teeth as sharp as razors,
Eyes as shiny as the moon,
Claws as sharp as knives,
A tail as long as Africa
And a body as big as China.

Add ears that look like mirrors,
Fur soft like a jumper.

Fergus Tinker (9)
Boxmoor Primary School

Firework Night

Fireworks, fireworks!
Bang! Whoosh! Flash!
Catherine wheels spinning as fast as a bullet from a gun,
Sparklers spitting as bright as the blazing sun,
Fireworks twisting like a roller coaster into the night sky,
Golden coloured like autumn leaves in the park,
Screamers whizzing at the speed of light,
Bangers darting like a golden shooting star.

Zoomers glittering over the watching crowd,
Beautifully coloured ones, blasting up like the speed of a speedboat,
Firecrackers exploding, sizzling through the night sky,
Blasting straight up like a roaring dragon,
Sparklers sizzling like a sausage in a hot pan,
Blasting as loud as an elephant,
Rockets darting just like a comet,
Fireworks, fireworks!

Jonathan Kilpatrick (10)
Cranborne Primary School

Tidal Wave

The tidal wave
It wiped out everything in sight
Humungous, turquoise splash
Like a roaring wave of wetness
Like a shouting angry sea monster
So terrifying when it rises and falls
Like you've died before it's happened
The tidal wave
Reminds me of a rocking boat
When it's on a storm.

Lauren Bartlett (11)
Cranborne Primary School

The Four Seasons

Summer, in the heat, with the roasting sun up ahead,
Children in swimsuits in the deep shimmering pool.
Flowers blooming red, blue and yellow,
Animals struggling to find a bit of shade,
Summer is fun and it'll be back next year.

Autumn's getting colder as the colourful leaves flutter to the ground,
Flowers starting to fade their beautiful colours,
Children jumping in the fallen leaves,
Animals starting to hibernate,
Autumn's fun and it'll be back next year.

Winter's here, it's freezing cold, as the freeze up rock solid,
It starts to snow, white the pavements turn, glistening white,
The trees turn completely bare as the temperature sinks below 0°C,
Children in the streets throwing snowballs here, there and everywhere,
Winter's fun and it'll be back next year.

Spring's here, the sun comes out and starts melting the snow
in the heat,
Daffodils sprouting in the dark earth,
Trees grow back their healthy leaves,
Animals of all sizes come out of hibernation to see around them,
Spring is fun and it'll be back next year.

Arthur Page (10)
Cranborne Primary School

Once Upon A Rhyme

T eaching brilliantly in all kinds of situations,
E ating only in the afternoon,
A lways working hard,
C onducting some orchestras that play excellently,
H ead teacher awards awarded to the well behaved,
E very day apart from the weekends is a school day,
R eally a lot of children play,
S ome like school, some don't!

Amar Patel (9)
Cranborne Primary School

Snow Has Come . . .

Snow has come, it's time to play,
Let's hop on our sledges and have fun today!

Have a great big snowball fight,
Until it is time for night.

Just watch it gleaming bright and white,
As it shimmers and shines through the night.

Sliding and gliding on the ice,
Oh snow is good, it's really nice!

School is out,
Without a doubt.

Building snowmen, what such fun,
Catch a snowflake on your tongue!

Snow is melting and going away,
I hope I'll see it another day.

Melissa Antoniou (9)
Cranborne Primary School

Life's Unfair

Why can't I have some stickers
Or even my favourite sweets, Snickers?
It's not fair!
Why do I have to go to bed at eight?
I'm not allowed to buy more fishing bait,
It's not fair!
Why can't I have school dinners?
Why can't I buy the skateboard for beginners?
Life's not fair!

Andrew Gibson (10)
Cranborne Primary School

Fireworks

A firework is fast
A firework is loud
A firework is pretty
And fireworks blast

What a fantastic sight
Though it gives small babies a fright
They bang, they screech and explode

As loud as an elephant
As fast as a jaguar
Darting like a shooting star
In the dark sky

As I watch them at my bedroom window
I look at the golden moon
Isn't it a lovely sight

I'll be going to bed soon
So goodnight bright moonlight.

James Brand (9)
Cranborne Primary School

Space

Space holds galaxies, stars and planets,
Shuttles and satellites are around the Earth,
For us to breathe, we have oxygen,
In space we have oxygen in suits,
The sun is in space,
We circle round every day, week and year,
On Earth gravity makes us stay on the ground,
In space there is no gravity, so we float around.

Ian Gunning (9)
Cranborne Primary School

Shoes

There are . . .
Big shoes, little shoes,
School shoes, training shoes,
High shoes, flat shoes,
Studded shoes, running shoes

And

Black shoes, coloured shoes,
Plain shoes, fancy shoes,
Clown shoes, baby shoes,
Teacher's shoes, smart shoes

Also

Clark's shoes, bowling shoes,
Laced shoes, buckled shoes,
Velcroed shoes and slip-on shoes.

Tansy Agnew (10)
Cranborne Primary School

The Possums

Possums, possums, hanging from a tree
He'd say, 'It belongs to me!'
At night he has a little hoot
In the morning he eats all his golden fruit

When it's winter, he's at his least
When it's spring, he's at his best
When he's hungry, he builds up his strength
'I wonder if I've grown any length?'

Possums, possums, the smallest one
They're as big as a bun
Possums are the special ones
They're as big as the smallest sun
They are the number one.

Matthew Lammas (9)
Cranborne Primary School

Firework Night

F ireworks racing into space,
I n the night zooming,
R emember the 5th of November,
E xploding up in the air like a bomb,
W hizzing, shooting, darting fast!
O range, red, yellow, green and colourful,
R aining down when it's done,
K ings of noise shooting in the air.

N ight as colourful as can be,
I see stars flying past,
G rowling, soaring, sparkling and screeching,
H igher than the moon, flying off Earth,
T rying to scream louder than before,
Bang! Bang! Boom!

Sophie Ferber (10)
Cranborne Primary School

Snow

Snow, snow gradually falling to the ground,
Making absolutely no sound,
Snow, snow gleaming bright,
Come and join the snowball fight.

Snow, snow melting in the sun,
The end of the day is here, but we had lots of fun,
Snow, snow glowing creamy white,
Still visible in the night.

Snow, snow on Christmas Eve,
Branches on trees, with no leaves.
Snow, snow will come to an end,
But it's going to come again.

Joshua Chan (10)
Cranborne Primary School

Fireworks

Fireworks darting through the sky like a shooting star
Blasting, twisting, whizzing
Whizzing at the speed of light
Crackle, whoosh, boom
Twisting like a roller coaster
Bang, sizzle, scream
Straight up like a bullet from a gun
Zoom, dart, twist
Colours, colours everywhere,
Shoot, blast, crash
Blazing like a summer's day
Zoom, soar, twist
All the colours of the rainbow
Scream, screech, bang
Golden like an autumn leaf
Pop, blast, spark
Fireworks finishing with a . . .
Bang!

Rachel Hillis (9)
Cranborne Primary School

A New Pet

My dad said we could have a new pet,
But check it was young from a vet.
Maybe a cat, rabbit or dog,
He said it could not be a frog.
Before I had a hamster who died in a week,
When he was buried I had a quick peek.
Dad said it had to be bigger than a cat,
So we would not lose it in a hat.
Now we're going to the RSPCA,
To get the new pet today.

Jack Mabbett (9)
Cranborne Primary School

Weather

Weather can make you happy,
Weather can make you sad,
Weather can make you ecstatic,
Weather can make you glad.

In the winter it might snow,
Slithering, sliding, quick and slow.
Racing here and racing there,
Snowball fights taking good care.

Snow trickling through your fingers
Like golden sand,
Wearing tight gloves
On your warm hand.

On a scorching hot day, go out to play,
On a cold night, snuggle up tight,
On a dull, gloomy day
The mist and air fills up with grey.

Wake up nice and early,
Sun shining bright,
Weather is fine
To fly a long-tailed kite.

Shahini Desai (9)
Cranborne Primary School

Sleepovers

I don't know why they're called sleepovers
All you do is stay up and chat
But if you're not careful, you might step on the cat
You might watch TV or you might laugh
And if you're really strange, you might get in the bath
One thing parents really don't like
Is children screaming in the middle of the night!

Laura Freedman (10)
Cranborne Primary School

Once Upon A Rhyme

Once upon a rhyme
Is about time
And how the world was made

With a drop here and over there
That was how the Earth was made

With a zoo of animals
What to do, I just don't know

With camouflaged colour
That's why the Earth
Isn't just a zoo

With plants and animals
Humans were born

So now the sun came up
And the moon went down
The dogs howled very loud

Once upon a rhyme
Is about time.

Thomas Ritson (10)
Cranborne Primary School

Snow

The snow is here all gleaming white
It shines and shivers all through the night
Sledges out, it's time to play
I think I'd like to build a snowman today

Icy roads and icy paths
Snow and ice
All over the grass

It's bedtime now
Time to end our play
I hope it snows another day.

Chelsie Richardson (9)
Cranborne Primary School

Animals

Animals live in the air, animals live everywhere,
Some live where it's hot, some live where it's cold,
Some live in the water and some live in a hole,
Some are cute, some are fluffy,
Some are pink and some can get huffy,
Lots can fly, lots can swim,
Some might look in your bin,
Some might roar, some might pounce,
Many can jump and some may bounce.

Humans are animals as plain as you can see,
Everyone is different like you and me,
Some animals are endangered because of us,
We need to stop this or the world will not
Be as beautiful as it is today.

James Fung (10)
Cranborne Primary School

Snow

Snow is glistening white
As if falls in the night
No one can stop snowball throwing
When it doesn't stop snowing
On the day it snows
Mums and dads change what they say
When it's time for school
I start being a fool.

Bradley Swaile (9)
Cranborne Primary School

Snow Day

Day off school
Kick a ball

School's out
Without a doubt

Snowmen here
Snowballs there

Yeah, yeah, yeah!

Sledging's fun
With water guns

Gingerbread men
And chocolate pens

Time to rest my sleepy head
In my cosy flower bed

In the morning back to school
Hope we're allowed in the swimming pool.

Nicole Hodges (10)
Cranborne Primary School

Spots

Spots, I'm seeing spots everywhere,
I'm seeing lots of these tiny little spots,
Yes it's true,
There are lots of little spots in the pans
And in the pots,
On the walls and in the halls,
With a fox and in a box
And they left little spots in the loo!
Spots!

Stephanie Jones (9)
Cranborne Primary School

Concentration Camp

Hidden behind a fence
Trapped by Germans
No hair left on my head
So scared I get no sleep
Dark bags under my eyes

I thought he was a good man
Took me for a shower
Trapped, locked door!
Can't get out!

On come the showers
But there is no water!
Just gas! Gas! Gas!

Help me, I was sacrificed
It's not fair
Millions of us had to die.

Emily Goldfinch (10)
Cranborne Primary School

Dreams And Nightmares

D ashing and daring dreams can be quite fun, although so can
R unning dreams in the bright morning sun, or
E lephants in a circus, ten girls riding one horse and
A man eating fire, quite scary of course, but
M agical dreams are the best I say,
S andy beaches with the Australian bay.

Now there is a dream which you'll need a friend,
A nightmare it's called, this is the end.

Rebecca Palmer (10)
Cranborne Primary School

Fireworks

As fast as a bullet from a gun,
Whizzing at the speed of light
And bright as the stars at night,
Bang! Whoosh! Crash!

As bright as a shooting star,
Lighting up the whole sky,
Going really fast and far,
Zooming up really high,
Zoom! Whish! Dosh!

People think it's a fantastic sight,
Blazing like a sun,
Very, very bright,
Boom! Whoosh! Zoom!

Paul Abdullah (10)
Cranborne Primary School

If

If teachers shout as loud as loud can be,
Then don't lose your temper,
At least not with me,
If you get told off
By the worst teacher ever,
Then don't shout back,
Absolutely never.

Jessica Crisford (10)
Cranborne Primary School

A Jew's War

Do you know how they treat us?
Chuck us around like a ball,
We are nothing but slaves here,
Nothing to live for at all.

Do you know how much they feed us,
The smallest slice of bread,
My ribs are showing through my skin,
They've even shaved my head.

Do you know what happens,
To those who are weak?
They are taken to a shower room
And there their deaths to seek.

Do you understand now
What Germans did to Jews?
Killing and watching us suffer,
Shouldn't make them amused.

Yasmin Laing (10)
Cranborne Primary School

The Mighty Sun

The mighty sun
It is as bright as a torch shining in your face
It is as hot as if you're sitting in a boiling volcano
It's high in the sky where nobody can reach
It is a precious thing to us
It is our only light
Without the sun
We would be like little ants being squashed.

Mino Petrasso (11)
Cranborne Primary School

Concentration Camp

I woke up one morning,
In a very unusual way,
I was taken away by soldiers,
As though I was their prey.

I was sent away to camp,
They shaved off all my hair,
The soldiers just stared and stared,
Just like they didn't care.

I was taken to the showers,
That's when I started to cry
And if you really want to know,
That's where I was to die.

Daniel Bellamy (10)
Cranborne Primary School

The Great Volcano

The great volcano
Kills anything in its path
Destructive, death threatening, phenomenal
Like a massive explosion,
Like boiling, lumpy orange juice,
Makes me feel like I'm being cooked,
The great volcano,
Makes me think of the boiling sun.

Andrew Nicolaou (10)
Cranborne Primary School

The Horrifying Storm

The horrifying storm
It can give you a painful death
Grey, grim, terrifying
Like the end of the world
Like the world is being killed
It makes me feel excited
Like I'm being lifted into the black night
The horrifying storm
When it's gone the world is terrorised
Like a new beginning.

Sophie Connor (10)
Cranborne Primary School

Rain

Rain is from far above
You are as beautiful as a dove
Some people say you've awful timing
So don't come out while the sun is shining
You're always here and always there
You spread it out so it is fair
Without you we would die
But we're glad when you say goodbye.

Laura Barnes (11)
Cranborne Primary School

The Great White Shark

I can swim underwater without holding my breath,
When little fish come near me they meet their death,
I can clamp my prey with my razor-sharp teeth,
When humans swim above me I drag them beneath,
Fear I can bring with one click of my jaw,
When humans see me they swim to shore.

Cara Allibone (10)
Cranborne Primary School

Sound

The tiniest sound in the world must be . . .
The sound of the trees rustling in the wind

The spookiest sound in the world must be . . .
The sound of a monster under your bed at night
With its friend the skeleton rattling itself about

The noisiest sound in the world must be . . .
The children at Cranborne School
Screaming in the playground

The happiest sound in the world must be . . .
Animals coming out of hibernation ready for spring.

Elizabeth Rowlands (7)
Cranborne Primary School

School

Some teachers are barmy,
Some teachers are fun,
Some will miss RE to let us play in the sun.

English, I'm not keen on,
Maths is a bore,
Art is my favourite of 2004.

Home time's the best,
Getting sweets from the tuck shop,
But don't eat too many or you'll go pop!

Jonathan Dixon (10)
Cranborne Primary School

The Moon

The moon is made of cheese!
At least that's what some believe,
For years it's been a mystery,
Sitting there as pretty as can be.
The moon is white,
The moon is gleaming,
The moon is gleaming white.
Craters all over the place,
The flags and footprints of astronauts,
It was made by God,
A sandwich it could be,
Between the Earth and sun,
As we spin in space.

Harry James (7)
Cranborne Primary School

If

If you think you're first piece is good
Then you're not getting anywhere
A good piece of work is one that doesn't just make you stare
If you think you're the drawing master
You're on the way to a disaster

If your pictures are in no way good
You're not on the way to artisthood
If you want to be an artist
Try, try, try!
That's the way to artisthood!

Tom Field (11)
Cranborne Primary School

Snow

Snow is cold
Snow is soft
Snow is white
Snow is slippery
Snow is everywhere
No school
Making snowmen
Throwing snowballs
Having fun
Snow hates hot
Snow melts when it sees the sun
Goodbye snowmen
Goodbye snow.

Jacob Andrews (8)
Cranborne Primary School

Whirlpool

Whirlpools are twisters in the sea,
Ships disappear to their awaiting graves,
A swirling magnet with destroying powers,
Swirling and twirling like a ballet dancer,
Whirlpools are Hell's gate,
The deceiving eye.

Tomas Cattini Moorcraft (11)
Cranborne Primary School

Flowers

Roses are nice,
Tastes like rice, covered in spice.

Tulips are beautiful,
Just like Miss G.

Sunflowers make myself,
As my mum waters them.

Buttercups shining on my neck,
Do like them . . .

Lilies are wonderful,
I want to be one.

Ashley Richardson (9)
Cranborne Primary School

Penguins

Penguins
Sliding on the ice
Swimming in the pools.
They huddle together
In Antarctica, the icy land.
Skidding together
These penguins
Are cool!

Ross Edwards (11)
Cranborne Primary School

Books

Books are for everyone
No one should be without one
I read lots and lots
I really don't know why
They're fun and interesting
I can be different people
Last week I found the Queen's jewellery
Yesterday I found some gold marbles
Tonight I'm hoping to be a secret agent
So come into the world of books like me!

Sriya Varadharajan (8)
Cranborne Primary School

Sound

The tiniest sound in the world must be
An ant marching on the pavement to its nest
The spookiest sound in the world must be
An owl howling in the night sky on the top of the house
The noisiest sound in the world must be
A rocket blasting to Neptune in space
The happiest sound in the world must be
The noise from football fans cheering when someone scores a goal.

Callum Turner (7)
Cranborne Primary School

Summer

Summer means hot
Summer means play and fun
Every day go to the beach to cool down
The sand twinkles gold in the sunshine
As it disappears into the sea
The deep blue sea
Sparkling like gold as lost as can be.

Emily Ferber (8)
Cranborne Primary School

Everybody

E is for everybody, like everyone is allowed to be different
V is for voice, everybody can speak
E is for everlasting, people last forever in our memories
R is for reality, something we live
Y is for young which everyone has been
B is for body, every organism has one
O is for organs that keep us alive
D is for dying when you come to the end of life
Y is for you, you're all very important.

Paris Daly (9)
Cranborne Primary School

Sounds

The tiniest sound in the world must be . . .
A newborn baby breathing,
The spookiest sound in the world must be . . .
A ghost singing in a dark graveyard,
The noisiest sound in the world must be . . .
The banging of a rock concert,
The happiest sound in the world must be . . .
Puppies snuffing as they snuggle up.

Heather Purton (8)
Cranborne Primary School

Spring Flowers

Buttercups and daisies
As sweet as sparrows
Pop their heads out to meet the sun
But no flowers are as beautiful
As a red rose in a green garden.

Sarah Papa (8)
Cranborne Primary School

Friendship

Friends are important,
Loyal and trustworthy,
My friend is,
She has neat and beautiful handwriting,
Is excellent at running, faster than me,
I don't care, she's my friend,
Everybody likes her,
Not just me,
She swims as fast as an eel,
Compared to my doggy paddle,
I don't care, she's my friend

Anytime I'm sad, she'll cheer me up,
Anytime I'm stuck, she'll help me out,
Anytime I'm hurt, she'll look after me,
She's my friend.

Can you see why?

Georgia Rose (9)
Cranborne Primary School

Sunset

At the end of the day
When the sun goes down
It leaves some lovely colours
Red, crimson, purple, pink and orange
I sit and stare in wonder

I sit and stare in wonder
Red, crimson, purple, pink and orange
It leaves some lovely colours
When the sun comes up
As another new day begins.

Paige Scrivener (8)
Cranborne Primary School

Stars In Space

Stars in the night twinkle, twinkle
Mars is as red as a rose
The sun is as bright as a sunflower
Earth spinning round and round
Moon going round, round the world
Jupiter, Mars, sun, moon, Earth, Neptune
Pluto, Uranus and the stars
Glittering in the night
All are in space.

Aneesah Laing (8)
Cranborne Primary School

Roses

Roses are red and sometimes pink
Roses will bloom and die
Roses will smile and smile
Until the sun goes down
Roses play in the great summer sun
Roses will sing like the choir
Roses will bloom in the summer
Roses will die in the winter but
Still roses are the prettiest flowers.

Emily Bannin (7)
Cranborne Primary School

A Friend

A is for anything, anything at all, that's what a friend would do for me
F is for friendly and funny
R is for respectful
I is for interesting
E is for everlasting
N is for nobody, nobody gets left out
D is for decent, you need a decent friend.

Claire Goldfich (8)
Cranborne Primary School

Sound

Spring has come, children come out to play
Just like the flowers popping their heads through the ground
We all enjoy pancake day
Soon be Easter
Weather getting warmer
We can go to the theme parks
Go on picnics
Birds are singing in their nests
Lambs being born and running around the green field
Spring has come.

Katie Barnes (7)
Cranborne Primary School

Summer

Summer means sunshine
Summer means heat
Everyone eats ice cream to cool down
Summer means shorts and T-shirts
Summer means swimsuits
Everyone goes swimming to cool down
We all love *summer!*

Madison Harrigan (8)
Cranborne Primary School

Snow Poem

The snow is sparkling
I love the snow
I like playing with snow.

Lauren Brooks (7)
Cranborne Primary School

Sounds

The tiniest sound in the world must be . . .
An ant creeping on the pavement

The spookiest sound in the world must be . . .
A ghost singing and playing the piano
Under a tree in a spooky graveyard

The noisiest sound in the world must be . . .
A drum in a band at a rock concert

The happiest sound in the world must be . . .
When a baby laughs.

Christos Loizou (8)
Cranborne Primary School

Snow

When I saw the snow
It looked like a show
It looked like a lot of fun
The poor sun
Snow you are so cold and light
But when the sun comes back
It will be a fright.

Hannah Sharp (7)
Cranborne Primary School

Snow Poem

Snow you are so soft
I just can't keep my eyes off you
You sparkle all around me
But no one has seen
I love you snow, goodnight.

Jade Murphy (7)
Cranborne Primary School

Wonderful Dolphins

Dolphins are so beautiful,
Swimming in the sea,
As they leap into the air,
They land so gracefully.

With people they're so popular,
When they see their happy show,
They swim around in circles,
Here and there they go.

Although the dolphins like to play
And seem as happy as can be,
I think they could be happier,
Just swimming in the sea.

Some dolphins are endangered
And sad our lives would be,
If the beauty of these creatures
We no more would ever see.

Melanie Lenihan (11)
Cromer Road School

My Wacky Gran!

My gran is very loopy,
She wears bloomers which are droopy,
She puts on make-up to go down town,
But if you ask me, she looks like a clown!
She asked me to rub her feet,
But believe me, they didn't smell sweet!
She climbed upon a roof,
Slipped and knocked out her rotten tooth,
She blew out the candles on her cake,
Lost her balance and fell in the lake!
Usually my gran is very funny,
But I hate it when she calls me 'Honey Bunny'!

Hayley Lines (10)
Cromer Road School

Snow

I woke up in the morning
Just as the day was dawning
Lots of snow lay on the ground
No speck of grass to be found

Mum told me there was no school
I thought this was really cool
Snowball fights were going on
Quick, before the snow has gone!

Angels and snowmen I made
They did not melt in the shade
Let's put my hat on its head
No, it's nearly time for bed!

Why are we coming inside?
Is it cos it's dark outside?
Take a look up in the sky
Snow is falling from up high!

How am I supposed to sleep
When the snow is falling deep?
I cannot wait one more day
I must go outside and play!

Jennie Croft & Hana Assadi (11)
Cromer Road School

Snow Poem

Snow falling,
Snow sparkling,
Snow falling, everyone's dancing,
Snow twinkling in the bright dawning day,
Snowflakes jumping, almost ready to lay,
Children tremble while they hold on to their hats,
While their hot lovely food lays steaming on their mats,
Then the cold little children come in and go to sleep,
While the white fluffy snow turns slowly into sleet.

Ellie Shipton (9)
Cromer Road School

Killer Truck!

Along the path this foul truck creeps,
Not far away from prey.
This truck could turn stone to plastic
And solid gold to clay!
Beware the killer truck!

The headlights flash like blazing stars
The message the truck brings is clear
The wheels make the ground vibrate
Kill anyone who's near!
Beware the killer truck!

Young Sammy Swashbucket
Approached the scene of the crime
Tripped in the path of the truck
But got out just in time.
Beware the killer truck!

Bob, Bill and Sergeant Sam
These are the town police.
They ran to the scene of the crime
And sighed with great relief
Because
A little boy was playing with his toy truck!

David Carey (9)
Cromer Road School

Simple Words

People's voices fill the air with a buzzy sound,
Words zooming up and down from the ceiling to the ground,
I spring up from my seat to catch hold of the words,
Trying to make sense of the things I have heard,
A hurricane of words tries to pull me in,
Bites of conversations crawl like bugs up my skin,
Adverbs chase verbs and adjectives chase nouns,
The confusion of the words is the lost and the found.

Carmen Thomson (10)
Cromer Road School

Who Am I?

Sitting in the corner with nothing to do
Staring blankly into space

Who am I?

'Do you want to play a board game
Or see what's on TV?'
But I just sit there glumly
While my father questions me.

Sitting in the corner with nothing to do
Staring blankly into space

Who am I?

My friend Sam is funny
And Fred is good at football
But me in my little corner
I have no talent at all.

Sitting in the corner with nothing to do
Staring blankly into space

Who am I?

My mum calls me in for breakfast
Cornflakes, milk and a crumpet
Then she turns round and says to me
'I've bought you a nice golden trumpet.'

Sitting in the corner with nothing to do
Staring blankly into space

Who am I?

I don't normally want to try out new things
'Cause I'm not very daring or gallant
But I still have a go at the trumpet
I think I have musical talent.

Ben Carey (9)
Cromer Road School

Winter

Wow it is so cold
My little fingers freeze
Shaking like a jelly
In the chilled winter's breeze
Snow is all around
Floating in the air
Settling on the ground
I am sinking down to my knees
While flakes silently dance
Between the trees
Happy children playing
Throwing snowballs and sleighing
Snowmen popping up
Don't let this winter fun stop.

Rosie Ann Gavan (7)
Cromer Road School

Love

Love is a teddy bear waiting for a hug.
Love is a red rose blossoming every day.
Love is chocolate, as sweet as it can be.
Love is a match made in Heaven.
Love is a flower smelling beautiful and fresh.
Love is a smile that never fades.
Love is about being together forever.
Love is like a butterfly that's colourful and bright.
Love is like a rainbow spreading across the sky.

Bhavisha Thaker (11)
Cromer Road School

A Child's Thoughts

At seven when I go to bed
I have such pictures in my head
Of magic power
Where a princess is locked within a tower
An enchanted garden covered with bright red roses
Which are watered with seven foot hoses
And kings and queens sit upon their thrones
That's what I see at seven when I go to bed

At seven when I wake again
I seek the magic land in vain
A scarf hung where the tower stood
A carpet hid the enchanted garden
And a doll's house sat where the castle was
That's what I seek when I wake again.

Ryan Searles, Tom Feldman & Sara Lumb-Evans (10)
Cromer Road School

Princess Fairy

Being a princess is the best thing ever,
I wouldn't give it up never,
Some people think that I'm scary
But what they don't know is that I'm a fairy,
I grant people's wishes,
Even if they want big, fresh, fat fishes,
I've got long blonde hair
And that is very rare,
So if you're in trouble,
I'll be there on the double,
Because I'm the *princess fairy!*

Andriana Voskou (11)
Cromer Road School

Birds

Birds have wings, feathers and beaks,
they lay eggs and they look after their chicks.

Birds live in all habitats,
on mountain tops, up trees and in deserts.
But birds like the pigeons
are found in all regions.

Some birds are large like the albatross and ostriches,
others are small like the partridges and finches.
The king of the birds is the eagle,
it is truly so regal.

Some birds don't like the light,
take the owl for instance,
it comes out at night.

Birds come in many colours,
red, blue and white.
Some of them have only one colour like
the green parrot and the red kite.

The flamingo is large and pink,
isn't that so strange you think?

The secretary bird for instance
is so fearless,
in the grass, it hunts for snakes.

Scientists think as they see birds soar
through the air that they are living dinosaurs.
Fancy the robin and warbler
being a relative of the velociraptor.

I sometimes watch birds if it's a sunny day
and when I'm older
I might write a book called 'Birds at Bay'.

Gareth Morgan (9)
Cromer Road School

The Show

Tightly attached around my neck,
I find a chain bringing me forward.
Watching the people laughing at me,
My keeper played a tune.

I didn't like being whipped,
So I started my routine.
Lifting my head and then my feet,
I began to dance for others' enjoyment.

I did my tricks,
I marched; then halted
And then I heard my keeper cry,
Now roly-poly somersault

And then I saw my keeper,
Going round with a begging cup,
Blushing through my big fur coat,
I heard the laughter stop.

I saw them pay something,
But they did not clap.
I wanted to stop playing tricks,
I wanted to go home to the distant forests.

My keeper was angry,
He whipped me and shouted,
Said we had bad business,
I didn't know what I had done wrong.

Beth Gainsborough (11)
Fleetville JMI School

Dancing Sunlight

Dappled sunlight dances,
Through unwoken leaves,
Once risen from their sleepy trances,
The leaves begin to sway
And start to sing in a mystical way.

Imogen Glover (11)
Fleetville JMI School

The Monsters Of The Dark

As soon as the lights were turned out once again,
The monsters of the dark crept out of their den.

Although I couldn't see them, I knew they were there,
Creeping around my room was their lair.

I heard their angry grunting, it made me shiver,
I knew that one day I could be their dinner!

I decided to turn on the lights, check them out;
I wanted to know what their game was about.

So I tiptoed to the lights and then flicked them on,
But I saw that the monsters of the dark were all gone!

Instead I saw my brother, grunting angrily on my floor,
I shouted, 'You do that to me, just once more!'

Grace Vance (9)
Fleetville JMI School

Feelings

Anger swept across the courtroom as
Happiness danced around the park
Loneliness longed for a friend as
Panic broke down and cried

Summer filled the world with joy
Winter with excitement
Autumn makes the world feel grumpy as
Spring makes us anxious.

Hannah Moghaddas (11)
Fleetville JMI School

Fire

Fire, fire
A big ball of fire
Round and round
Watch out, it's on the ground

Fire, fire,
It's getting hot now
Let it out
There is no need to panic or shout!

Fire, fire
Orange, yellow and red
I'm feeling hotter
It's going up the stairs
Soon it will catch my bed

Fire, fire
A big ball of fire
Round and round
Watch out, it's on the ground.

Shahnaj Haque (8)
Fleetville JMI School

Fruity Limerick

There was an ambitious young fig
Who took a small grape to a gig
He tripped her over
So she went back to Dover
And told him to eat with the pigs.

Emily Kay (10)
Fleetville JMI School

The King Of Quizzical Island

(Inspired by 'The King of Quizzical Island' by Gordon Snell)

The king of Quizzical Island
Had a most inquisitive mind,
He said, 'If I sail to the edge of the world,
I wonder what I'll find?'

So he sailed up the acid waterfall
And then he zoomed down,
He found himself in Topsy Turvy Town,
Where everyone wears a crown.

So he walked along the chequered front walks,
Wondering what to do,
He saw a bubble boat,
That gave him a clue.

That night he hijacked a bubble boat
And went to the waterfall,
He sped up and made a plunge,
He made it, he felt proud and tall!

Stefan Maile (10)
Fleetville JMI School

Fruity Limerick

There was an attractive young pear,
Who grew a new style of hair,
It reached down to the floor,
But got trapped in the door,
So that style of hair did tear!

Rachel Kay (9)
Fleetville JMI School

What Shall I Do Today?

What shall I do today?
I know, I'll do ballet,
Or maybe I'll mix sugar and spice,
But that in your sandwich is not always nice.
There's always rugby, I'm not sure about that,
'Cause last time I played, I tripped over a cricket bat.
My brother's playing a very good game,
Me, oh me, I feel the pain,
My mum has called me up to bed,
Now I've got a pain in the head.
I'm all snuggled up tight,
My mum slips in and says goodnight!

Rebecca Tough (8)
Fleetville JMI School

My New Pet

I went to the pet shop to buy a pet,
I went round the cornor and suddenly met . . .
A mad professor making a bet.

'I bet I can invent a new animal,' he said
'An animal will be fine,'
Said a man in clothes of the colour lime.

They both spotted me and beckoned me over,
'Come choose an animal,
Describe it and we'll make it.'

I said, 'I want a pet please, pink and purple,
I want a little lion that is tame.
Who does not get too big
And has a fluffy mane,
That is my pet to be.'

So they put my wants into a machine
And now I have that pet called Wonder,
The answer to my dream.

Jessica Hazrati (10)
Garden Fields JMI School

Monkeys!

Monkeys are so sweet,
cos they have soft feet,
swinging branch to branch
and gracefully dance,
in the moonlight,
on a warm night.

In the jungle playing,
all day long, sunbathing
in the boiling sun,
eating tons of buns,
laughing out loud
and making lots of sound.

Their big smiling faces,
peeping through their hiding places,
I love monkeys!

Lauren Richardson (11)
Garden Fields JMI School

Footie Fever

I knew a boy called Wart,
Footie was his favourite sport,
Then he caught footie fever,
We took him to the doctor
And the doctor said, 'No more footie for you!'
So now Wart's caught disco disease.

Peter Naughton (11)
Garden Fields JMI School

A Snowy Poem

The snowflakes fall down on the frozen paths and pavements
The snow is very cold, so you need to wrap up warm
The snow is fluffy, all of a glow . . .
Not mashed potato but white crispy snow
Swirling and swirling, round and round
No sound is made when the snow comes down
Crunch, crunch, under your feet
The sound made when the snow's been resting all week
Swirling like a kaleidoscope, the snow falls softly on the slope
We'll soon be skiing, sleighing and more playing in the snow
Till half past four
We sit on the sleigh ready to go
Hurtling at speed, where will we stop? Nobody knows.

Rebecca Newman (9)
Garden Fields JMI School

Roller Coaster Ride

When I went on a roller coaster,
It was fast and quick,
I brought along my poster,
My brother brought his stick,
He nearly poked his eye out,
But he missed and poked his thigh,
My mum and dad were worried
And so was I!

Abigail Hazrati (8)
Garden Fields JMI School

Playground, Playground

P layground, playground with lots of fun
L aughter, joy and everyone
A ngry kids, sad kids, everyone's there
Y o-yos and skipping ropes
G ather round, chitter-chatter
R ound and round the girls go
O ut in the fresh air
U nder the hot sun
N ever miss play
D own on the playground kids play.

Esme Rice (9)
Garden Fields JMI School

Clown Poem

Clowns are funny, clowns are sad,
Clowns are good and clowns are bad,
They throw buckets of water and custard pies
And spray paint and foam in each other's eyes.

They wear lots of make-up and a painted grin,
They juggle with balls and make plates spin,
Clowns have coloured hair and a big red nose
And drive a rickety car which never goes.

Amy Ordinaire (10)
Garden Fields JMI School

Pony Poem

P onies are perfect in every way
O n their backs I ride each day
N aughty ponies buck and jump
Y ou can easily topple and fall with a bump!

Lucy Sanderson (10)
Garden Fields JMI School

Fish!

I wish I was a fish
My tail would swirl and swish!
Blowing bubbles in the tank
People drop food in with a twank!

I wish I was a fish
My fins would twirl and swish!
Yummy food blue and green
My friends are rather clean!

I would be called Midema
I would be such a dreamer
Floating everywhere
With the fish castle a bit bare!

The algae on the fish tank glass
I'll think you'll have to have a fish tank pass!
Everyone staring in at me on my brick bike
I wonder what a fish life would be like?

Tess Carey (10)
Garden Fields JMI School

Winter

W inter is cold
I cy winds blow
N ever a sunny day
T omorrow more snow
E very day is just like the last
R oll on summer, roll on fast!

George Williams-Gunn (7)
Garden Fields JMI School

Fish In The Sea

Fish in the sea
Fish in the sea
Swimming round and round me

Fat ones, thin ones
Some that spin ones

Fish in the sea
Fish in the sea
Swimming round and round me

Some in twos, some in threes
Some that hide behind the trees

Fish in the sea
Fish in the sea
Swimming round and round me

Good ones, bad ones
Some that are sad ones.

Ella Brown (8)
Garden Fields JMI School

Who Am I?

My ball is really cool
I kicked it against the wall
Football is the best
I'll always pass the test
Because football is my game
Now try to guess my name!

Madison Warbey (8)
Garden Fields JMI School

Once Upon A Rhyme

Once upon a time,
There was this little rhyme,
It started with a boy,
Who always played with his toy,
He was getting ready for bed,
Till he suddenly lost his ted,
He was crying all night,
It was not a pleasant sight,
He was alright in the morning,
But he always kept yawning,
All of his friends came,
Asking him if he wants to play a game.

May Muhtadi (10)
Garden Fields JMI School

Fairies

There once was a fairy,
Her name was Mary,
She had very tickly toes
And a very, very small nose.

She had very long hair,
Which was quite blonde and fair,
She lived in a house,
With a small pet mouse.

Catherine Cole (8)
Garden Fields JMI School

Going To The Zoo

I like going to the zoo
I love to hear the cows go moo
All the penguins look so cute
The mice are really, really minute
I like to hear the lions roar
I like to see the wild boar
The monkeys swing from tree to tree
I'd like to bring one home with me
I like to see the wolves howl
I like to see the leopards prowl
I like going to the zoo
Maybe next time you would like to come too?

Flora McCluskey (10)
Garden Fields JMI School

My Friends

My friends are always there for me,
I have two best friends, one's a she and one's a he,
I'm always in the park playing with them,
They even bought me a big, big gem,
My friends are cool, my friends are great,
They'll both turn out to be a great, great mate.

Nicola Tinker (10)
Garden Fields JMI School

Hugs And Kisses

Big hugs and little hugs all day long,
Means so much to me and you,
Having so much fun.

I hug Mummy, Daddy, baby brother,
As well as my cousins, big and small,
Uncles, aunties, grandma, grandpa, friends of course,
That's who I like to hug.

I love to kiss my teddy bear at night,
Oh and of course my dolls,
So they don't get a fright,
On a spooky night.

Rosalind Bennett (6)
Garden Fields JMI School

Mountains

Mountains are very tall
Sometimes I think they will fall
Some of them have snow
The avalanches always flow
The Alps is a mountain range
Sometimes mountains change
For instance there are volcano mountains
The lava shoots out in fountains
Mount Everest is very high
When you get to the top, you might even die.

Michael Johnson (10)
Garden Fields JMI School

Harry Potter

Harry goes to Hogwarts school,
Where he learns how to duel and transfigurate too,
Professor Dumbledore is the Head
And Hagrid the game keeper lives in a shed,
There's no escaping Snape's mean ways
And Quidditch is what Madame Hooch plays,
He buys all his equipment from Diagon Alley,
Where he may find a broomstick rally,
At the end of the year when it's time to go home,
The Durselys leave him all alone.

Ruth Ferguson (11)
Garden Fields JMI School

Winter Is Coming

It's very cold and it's near December
It's like a block of ice
It's snowing as white as a sheep
No one wants to go outside
I'm so excited because it's nearly Christmas
All the presents under the tree
I wish I could open them.

Kimberley Chowdhary (8)
Garden Fields JMI School

Trundle Like A Truck

Trundle like a truck,
Stretch like a limousine,
Driving around the lovely
Beautiful mountain scene.

Zooming like a car,
Bobbing like a boat,
Some people say,
'Cars don't float.'

Chugging like a tractor,
Puffing like a train,
All the passengers scream,
When there's a big hurricane.

Roaring like a motorbike,
Gliding like an aeroplane,
The pilot's name is
Uncle Billy Wayne.

Edward Rose (8)
Garden Fields JMI School

Cats

Cats can be big
Cats can be small
Cats can be nice
Or not nice at all

Cats' eyes are thin
Cats' colours are bright
Cats' whiskers are short
Cats' mouths are tight

Cats can be happy
Cats can be sad
Cats can be good
Cats can be bad.

Danielle Chowdhary (11)
Garden Fields JMI School

The Summertime

In the summertime
The food is so fine
Summer nights are so calm
You could even have a holiday on a farm
Or a holiday in the sun
And have lots of fun
While you're in the swimming pool
You could be somewhere cool
You'll never have spare time on your hands
While you play in the golden sand
It's all up to you
All you want to do
It will be heaven for you and your family
You'll be happy together
So don't worry
There is no hurry
You'll have fun all day
You'll have fun all the way
In the summer.

Amy Huckle (10)
Garden Fields JMI School

Mum/Flower

M ums are always there for you
U nder every heart there is the love of a mother
M ums are special to everyone

F lower is a beauty
L ong and tall, different colours
O n summer days flowers grow beautifully
W here? Over there is a flower
E verywhere are flowers that come from seeds
R eally a flower is special to everyone.

Khushboo Rafeez (9)
Garden Fields JMI School

Accordion Exam

My body was sweating,
My heart was pumping,
Pull yourself together,
Just please stop fretting!

Waiting in the plastic chair,
Waiting for my turn,
I thought back to when I started music,
The day I began to learn.

My knees were knocking vigorously,
Like an unstable tree,
All of a sudden I heard a voice,
'Next pupil, Faye Ventre.'

I gathered up my courage
And pushed my bellows shut,
I walked into the music room
And heard my sister tut.

The door closed,
I sat down,
I then noticed,
The examiner frown.

45 minutes passed slowly by,
I walked from the room, feeling rather glad,
As I floated outside, without a word,
I thought, *not all examiners are that bad.*

Faye Ventre (10)
Hatfield Heath CP School

Nobody Cares

Nobody cares
About animals dying,
Poachers killing,
Animals crying.

Tigers are hunted,
For their fur,
So people can look posh,
Now we can't hear them purr.

Crocodiles are hunted,
For their scaly skin,
To make handbags,
Crocs are just being thrown in the bin.

Baby seals are hunted,
For their furry coats,
To make rugs,
Being killed by blokes.

Chloe Pepper (10)
Hatfield Heath CP School

Stop Fighting!

Mum and Dad are fighting,
I'm hiding in my room,
I can hear Mum crying,
This is the night of doom.

I'm too scared to go downstairs,
Mum is really worried
'Cause when Dad goes away,
It'll be extremely horrid.

Oh no! I hear the door slam!
Why can't I hear them fight?
Dad, where are you going
In the middle of the night?

Hannah Leech (10)
Hatfield Heath CP School

I Wish

I wish I had a friend
Someone that I would play with
I wish I wasn't on my own every day
It drives me round the bend
I wish I was invited to a sleepover
Or a party of some kind
Why do I get bullied?

I wish I had someone that I could share my secrets with
I want someone to hold me when I fall
I can't stand it anymore
Sometimes I want to push myself
O
 V
   E
      R
      A
      C
      L
      I
      F
      F.

Abbi Smith (11)
Hatfield Heath CP School

The Snowman

Our snowman
Is the biggest in the world
It has a giant orange nose
And a big pipe
Our snowman
Has a top hat
And buttons of coal

Our snowman watches over our garden
Like a guard
He protects our house
From any type of danger

I wake up in the morning to look out the window
Expecting to see
A snowman with a big orange nose and a big top hat.

Jamie Stevens (10)
Hatfield Heath CP School

The Fear

I was in a car
Driving really fast
The roof was down
Loud music in the night
I was in a fight
I saw a light
It was really bright
I went past it
And the car stopped
I almost came out of the car
I didn't have my seatbelt on
So I smashed my head.

Billy Norris (10)
Hatfield Heath CP School

The Ogleebog

'Beware my son of the Ogleebog,
It blunders waiting in the fog;
It'd like to eat your hoppletoo,
Or maybe, if it feels like it, even you!'

'I know!' John said, 'I'll be fine,
Now I'll use the toilet, if you don't mind.'
'But Son, that is where the Ogleebog lurks,
Going there is a job for murks!'

But John did not care at all,
For which his father called him a fool,
So John went to the toilet to see him off,
But instead out came the Ogleebog to bite his head off!

Sebastian Dixon (11)
Hatfield Heath CP School

My Poem

I'm a poet and I didn't know it
I know I'm a good fighter
But I didn't know I was a good writer
My sister thinks not
My mum thinks I'm good
My dad thinks I'm brilliant
And I think *what!*

I can't wait till my poem is took
Into a book
It will look great covered in lights
With tinsel dangling down
And my book shining bright.

Sarah Jones (11)
Hatfield Heath CP School

Home From School

I can see my mum cooking curry as I see it glow
My dad watching an action James Bond film
Shadows so dark I want it to go
The TV on from upstairs with my sister
I can hear my sister break a glass and I nearly get a blister
My sister shouting, 'I want to watch Top of the Pops!'
My sister putting on her make-up
I hear three telephones ringing
And my mum is singing
I can taste curry melting in my mouth
And fish sizzling
I can taste Coca-Cola, very fizzy
I can see my sister making me spin and I feel very dizzy
My dad drinking beer
And my mum shouting to my sister about why she broke the glass
My dad putting his volume to max on his mouth
And tells my sister to go to her room
I find my football, very old
I kick the ball very hard and actually felt my foot was gone
I went inside feeling really cold
Then I saw my dad shouting, *'Goal!'* as he watched TV.

Eren Akademir (9)
Hatfield Heath CP School

Home From School

I can see grass flooding like it was in space
People on their land racing past like cheetahs
More and more bonfires flickering in the air like mad

I'm listening to owls hooting their heads off
Cars speeding past like mad as a monkey

I can taste the smell of roast dinner
I can smell smoke from the oven
I can touch hot plates as hot as the sun.

Nicholas Bell (8)
Hatfield Heath CP School

Home From School

I can see my mum cooking chicken soup,
I can see my dad playing games on the computer,
I can see my brother just coming through the door.

I can hear sizzling of tea,
I can hear keys clicking and the mouse moving.

I can taste bacon in the air from yesterday's dinner,
I can taste the rabbit's food, it is disgusting.

I can touch the fur on the floor where the rabbits have been,
I can touch bumpy walls in the kitchen,
I can touch soft tables in the bedroom.

I can smell my rabbit's food,
I can smell the dinner, it smells very nice,
I can smell nail polish where my mum painted her nails.

Naomi Bartram (8)
Hatfield Heath CP School

Home From School

As I get in the silver Renault
I can see well-painted houses,
The grass growing for the spring
And trees going away behind us
And I can also see the mud tracks where the tractor has been.

I can hear my mum asking the other two how their day's been,
Then when she asks me, I reply, 'It could have been better.'

I taste fresh air whilst the window is open
And the wagon wheel that I will have when I get in.

I touch the glass window while I stare out into space,
While I touch the silky book bag.

When I am in the front, I can smell my dog's fur
And the wood of the shoe and coat cupboard.

Harry Beeching (8)
Hatfield Heath CP School

Home From School

I've come inside the door and I see . . .
The TV blaring out full volume
My brother greeting me
My mates are at the front door asking if I can come out to play
My baby brother cries, 'Mummy he is teasing me!'

I can hear the birds singing peacefully
My mum's horrible singing!
My mother shouting like a madman!
Dog barking her head off
Will it ever stop?
Dinner time! I taste the burgers
Not to mention the fries
My dad is eating curry
'Roast tomorrow!'
Yum-yum!
I feel the PlayStation 2 controls
Playing The Simpson's Hit and Run
I'm holding the knife and fork
Chicken on the fork
And the soft skin of my brother

I smell the peas in the oven
Hot!
Along with the chips
Pasta too
Chocolate cake
Mmmm!

Alfie Bond (8)
Hatfield Heath CP School

Home From School

My cousin comes round and she is only one,
I pick her up and sit her on the sofa with some toys,
She sits and plays, but when she gets bored
She makes a moaning sound,
I pick her up and put her down.

She toddles to the music room and plays with the plastic food,
Then she sees the piano and says, 'Up, up' and stands up.
I open the lid and she starts playing -
What a dreadful sound!

I can smell Olivia's food - it's horrible.
I carry Olivia and sit her at the table.
She eats her horrible food and then it's time for my dinner.

My dinner was lovely - it was pasta, no sauce.
My brother hates it, but I adore it.

Olivia grabs my hand,
Her hand feels gooey where she has stuck her hand in her mouth.
My hand was now the same -
My hand now feels gooey too!

Harriet Bellieu-Cruse (9)
Hatfield Heath CP School

Jellyfish Haiku

Some are in box form,
You don't want to go near them,
Cos they sting like hell.

Freddie Shaw (10)
Hatfield Heath CP School

Home From School

When I get home from school
I go up into the playroom and play with my Lego
I put the TV on and when I'm playing with my exciting Lego
Then I get bored

So I go downstairs and ask my nan, 'What are you doing?'
And I could smell roast dinner and cakes baking in the oven
After that I smell ice cream with large toppings on it

And sometimes Lewis beats me up
I play with my Star Wars set
Then I go upstairs and play a game called Eye Toy
And you can see yourself on the TV
You can do karate on Eye Toy
And my highest score is 4580
You get a photo if you get a higher score than me
You could do boxing
And you can play against a robot called Robro

Then I go down and watch 'I'm A Celebrity Get Me Out Of Here'
Then I go to bed
And I look dead!

Reece Colella (9)
Hatfield Heath CP School

Home From School

I can hear the stress around the house
That turns into havoc and scares the mouse

And the taste of the cool ice cream that sticks to my mouth
That melts in three seconds without a doubt

And the luscious food on the table
Oops sorry Mum, the food's all gone from the table!

When I come home from school
Things are such a mess
I can't even find my desk!

Luke Marioni (8)
Hatfield Heath CP School

Home From School

I can see cars driving past our house,
I can see Noah running and tripping and starting to cry.
I can see my mum coming downstairs and saying what has happened
And Noah telling her.
I can hear Noah playing with his Action Men,
I can hear Bethan shouting (as usual),
I can hear Digestive tweeting lots of words but in birdy language
So I do not understand a word.
I can taste my dinner being cooked
And Bethan's strawberry Sleeping Beauty doll and Digestive too,
I can touch my lovely soft sheet,
I can touch my mum's skin when she puts me to bed,
I can touch my lovely teddies' fur when I cuddle them.
I can smell pollen from the flowers
And my mum and dad's strong cup of coffee,
I can smell the cherry tree.

Hannah French (8)
Hatfield Heath CP School

Home From School

When I get home from school
I can see my brother getting out of the blue minibus
I can spot my mum getting cross, she's making a fuss!
I can listen to the TV in the background
And I can hear my music, it's really loud!
I can hear my brother ringing the doorbell a million times
Because he's in a bad mood most of the time!
I can taste my cat's food from the living room
And I can taste an awful smell, it's like perfume!
I can touch my cat's lovely black shiny fur
I chase it upstairs and I can feel my pillow that's lying there
I can smell Mum making our tea
And I can just about smell Mum making her coffee!
Our house makes such a noise
I think it's all because of the boys!

Katy Crewe (9)
Hatfield Heath CP School

Home From School

Daisy came to greet me,
When I came home from school.
I can see my sister watching TV,
My mum walking through the hall -
I pass my lunch box on.

I can hear my sister shouting
And Daisy purring louder.
Daisy jumps into my arms
And the feel of her fur is soft and warm.

I can smell Daisy's cat food,
Then I can smell my mum cooking toasties,
I can smell Daisy's fur lingering on my hands.

I taste my lovely dinner made by my mum,
I can imagine Daisy's cat food, it tastes really bad!

I am touching Daisy's little running boots that are her paws.

Suddenly her claws spring out and she's clinging to my jumper,
I gently throw her off.

Nicola Durkin (8)
Hatfield Heath CP School

Home From School

I can see my sister playing with her dolls.
I see my mum in the kitchen making lunch.
I am now in my room doing my homework.

I can hear my mum playing the piano,
I can hear my sister jumping around the bedroom.

I am in the village on my bike -
Flicking my bell going *cling, cling, cling.*

I can taste the sandwiches on the kitchen table,
I am in the front room waiting for lunch,
With my sister shouting, 'I want my lunch!'
She forgot to say please or thank you.

Abigail Grantham (8)
Hatfield Heath CP School

Walking Home From School

I can see shire horses in a field
And mostly Ford Focuses whizzing straight past
My freezing cold feet
German Shepherd dogs and tabby cats running by
Flaming hot streetlight flickering on

I can hear stallion horses and German Shepherd dogs
Making wonderful sounds together
Tabby cats are purring saying let me through
I want to join in with my animal friends
I can still hear the cars whizzing by

I can taste the wonderful smell of McDonald's
Just directly opposite me
The dinner's in the oven
And the cake we made this morning

I can touch my coldish knife and fork
And my warm bottle of Ribena drink
I can also touch boiling hot gravy swirling around my delicate finger

My sister is beside me squeezing my hand
So my blood cannot fit through the gap
But I love her very much!

Emma Fisk (8)
Hatfield Heath CP School

Home From School

As I enter my house I can see
My mum making a wonderful tea
My sister trying on clothes in front of the mirror
Trying to get thinner and thinner
My cats lay on the sofa, cute as can be
But wait, no, they're going to rest on my knee

I can hear my sister singing really badly
And also my cats purring really gladly
My mum's getting angry phone calls that drive her up the wall
And now my sister's listening to full sound Sean Paul

I can smell my mum's rose perfume lingering from last night
And the fumes of the polish make her feel itchy and tight
I can smell the jelly food that makes me sick
And can smell my cat bringing in a mucky stick

And last but not least I can feel my new, tidy, comfy, cosy bed
Zzzzz.

Francesca Fox (8)
Hatfield Heath CP School

Hollywood

It starts off as a dream
That gets bigger and bigger
Auditions, adverts, sitcoms
Then finally
Hollywood
London, New York, Paris or Rome
Why Hollywood?
Hollywood, Hollywood
Lights, camera, action
Hollywood.

Charlie Knight (10)
Hatfield Heath CP School

Home From School!

As I stepped into the hallway of my house,
I could see my sisters racing to get the TV control first,
I can see them thumping and fighting.

I can feel the cold air coming from the open door behind me
And the cold smooth door handle of my room,
It is freezing my hand,
I can feel my red pencil I am using for my homework.

I can smell the strong scent of my mum's perfume
And my mum's cup of tea,
I can smell the leftover chilli from the night before.

I can taste the cheesy pasta cooking in the oven
And heavenly chocolate melting in my mouth.

I can hear the booming TV
And my mum telling my younger sister to tidy her room.

Charlotte Hill (8)
Hatfield Heath CP School

The Band

There was a man from Fairland,
Who was the conductor of a band,
He needed a helping hand,
So he decided to expand.

They were always on the move,
They had the best grooves,
They were so smooth,
But they could still improve.

Lloyd Hammett (11)
Hatfield Heath CP School

Home From School

I see the large tree outside my house
I see the door open wide and
Nan with her arms outstretched ready to give me a cuddle
I see the ingredients ready to be made into a cake

I hear Nan asking me what my day has been like
I hear my brother turning the radio on loud
I hear Mum getting the cake tin ready

I smell my mum beating the cake mixture
I smell the cake cooking in the oven
I smell the cake waiting to be eaten

I taste the fruit in the warm cake
I taste the butter as it dribbles down my chin
I taste the coldness of my glass of water

I touch the empty plate and glass
I touch the remote control . . .

Dennis Gregory (9)
Hatfield Heath CP School

Audi

Audi in the light
Speeding round like a kite
Silver and black
I don't mind because I love my Audi.

Gareth Clifford (11)
Hatfield Heath CP School

Home From School

As I come home from school, I can see
The chickens charging about in the run
I can see the ducks swimming on the freezing cold pond

I can hear the very noisy engine on the tractors in the field
I can hear the ducks quacking away as I come down the drive

I can taste the sausages and the chips my mum is cooking
I can taste the salt on the crisps my sister is eating

I can touch my guinea pig
And I can feel the prickly straw in the cage

I can smell the fields being harvested in the summer
With the big combine and I can smell oil on my dad
When he comes in from work!

And when I come in, oh no, here comes my sister
To give me a great big hug!

Laura Grieve (9)
Hatfield Heath CP School

The Boogieman

What was that noise?
Was it my mum or was it a monster?
The floorboards creak and in comes the . . .
Boogieman!
He jumps on my bed, I am filled with dread,
He starts cutting off my head,
He sucks out my brain and I am in pain,
He puts his finger up my nose and pulls out something green!

Jordan Baker (10)
Hatfield Heath CP School

Likes, Fears And Dreams

I like to walk along the beach,
Just as a teacher likes to teach,
I like to walk along a stream,
Just as everybody has a dream,
I like to eat a lot of food,
Only when I'm in the mood.

I fear the monster under my bed,
Every night as I lay down my head,
What was that noise?
Was it my dad
Or was it the dinner I just had?

I dream to be in a world of chocolate,
Where your mum doesn't call, 'What's in your pocket?'
I would like to be in a world of sweets,
Where your mum doesn't have to clean your sheets.

Ross Williams (10)
Hatfield Heath CP School

Travelling Dreams

It drifted slowly across the sea,
Wow, I thought it could not be,
A voice in the wind,
A whistle in the waves,
The dream, I thought, *it's coming to me!*

It trickled down into a stream
And slid down a sunbeam,
Over the rainbow,
Through rustled leaves,
The dream I thought, *it's coming to me!*

It danced slowly through the air,
Up to the Arctic, past a polar bear,
Down with the waterfall,
Seeking the shade in a flower's petals,
It was here, the dream was here!

Claire Fisk (10)
Hatfield Heath CP School

Home From School

I can see my dad in his armchair who can never get out of it,
My mum doing her exercise,
My brother leaping on his bed,
My lobster gulping all the fish,
My electric scooter trashing the house.

I can hear music making the ceiling groove,
My dad switching channels,
People digging outside my house,
Cars zooming down the street.

I can taste beefburgers burnt,
The smell of fresh air as the windows rise,
Cans of apple juice,
Bowls of sweet popcorn.

I can feel the beat of music,
I can touch the bubbling bubbles,
I can touch the sprinkle of water.

I can smell hot peppers spicing,
I can smell smoke coming out of the smoky oven.

Billy Irvin (9)
Hatfield Heath CP School

My Dogs

My dogs are fun
They run and run
They like to eat
Lots of meat
They always bark
And run in the dark
They like to play
On a windy day.

Sam French (11)
Hatfield Heath CP School

Home From School

As I got home from school I can hear the guinea pigs squeaking
George shouting
George watching a video with the volume up too high
And my mum starting to sigh.

I can smell the guinea pigs' cage, not very nice
The washing on the line
And my dad's burp from his behind!

I can feel the guinea pigs' hair as soft as a pillow
And the carpet bumpy and rough.

I can see my mum turning off the PlayStation
And my brother being sent up to his room.

I can taste the mouth-watering spaghetti Bolognese
That my mum had cooked
And the freezing cold ice cream.

Lydia Logan (9)
Hatfield Heath CP School

Home From School

H urrying through the door,
O n goes the light,
M um hands me a drink,
E mpty is the glass now.

F avourite programme is on the TV,
R ushing to turn it on,
O n the floor I sit,
M um tells me it's too loud.

S uddenly it's time for tea,
C hips, sausages and beans,
H urray! Mum knows what I like,
O n the way to bed now,
O h I must remember to feed my guinea pig tomorrow,
L ights turned off at eight o'clock.

Emma Newman (8)
Hatfield Heath CP School

Home From School

When I get home from school my brother runs upstairs with
Things he brought down
My cat sits there on the window sill waiting for me to let
Him in the house

I can see my mum putting on the kettle
My brother screams loudly every time I come home from school for me
To play with him -
If I don't, I'm dead or he drives me insane!

I can touch my two bouncy sofas in the living room,
My wet towel drying in the bathroom,
I can smell my mum cooking our tea in the kitchen,
My mum has flowers that smell nice and sweet.

Our mum calls us for tea and afterwards we watch The Simpsons
Then we have our dessert - that is sweet,
Then we go to bed and it smells of nice smells,
When I get up in the morning I feel a bit grumpy!

Glenn Jackson (9)
Hatfield Heath CP School

The Worm

The worm, the worm
Could only squirm
It couldn't walk
Or talk

He couldn't swim
And he couldn't win
A single race
With his slow pace

He couldn't kick a ball
Or do anything at all
He didn't move fast
So at last
He was squashed.

Sean Wearden (11)
Hatfield Heath CP School

Home From School

I can see my sister playing with her dolls
My pet guinea pigs running around in their messy cage
I can see my mum cooking the evening meal
My sisters playing outside
I can see my bedroom all messy and cramped
While my dad is watching the telly!

I can hear my guinea pigs squeaking
My next-door neighbour's owl hooting
I can hear my sisters screaming loudly
The trees in my garden swaying
I can hear my dad whistling
While the grass keeps on blowing!

I can smell the food my mum is cooking
The smell from the car's petrol
I can smell the soap from the bathroom
The perfume my mum is wearing!

Emily Long (9)
Hatfield Heath CP School

A Race Of Old Men

There was a race of old men,
The winner got a hen,
They got a bruise,
When they sleepwalked while they snoozed.

They ran into a pool,
It was a bit too cool,
They got back out
And they died with a shout.

None of the old men
Were close to winning the hen,
They gave a shout and fell down dead,
But the organisers had an idea in their head.

Christopher Bell (11)
Hatfield Heath CP School

Home From School

I can see my brother playing on his Game Boy,
I can see my mum cooking her lovely Bolognese,
My dad is on his boring computer,
My cat leaning against my leg,
I can see the bubbles bubbling over the saucepan.

I can hear the click-click-clicking of the computer's mouse,
I can hear my cat miaowing,
I can hear my brother getting told off.

I can smell the cat food
And carrots in the saucepan.

I can touch my soft pillow,
My squashy duvet,
My cuddly teddies,
My magazines.

I can taste the Bolognese my mum is cooking,
Wafting in the air!

Chloe Scott (9)
Hatfield Heath CP School

Man's Best Friend

My friend, Matt, drives me round the bend,
He says technology's man's best friend,
He talks about it every day,
'Technology is the best,' he'd say.

'Computers, radios, the TV too,
They're so intelligent like me or you,
Soon it'll be here all the time,
Help stop bandits, crooks and crime.'

He'd say, 'Come on Ollie, listen to me,
If I keep telling you, soon you'll see,
The future's now, the future's set!'
I'd reply, 'I'd prefer a pet.'

Oliver Hancock (11)
Hatfield Heath CP School

Home From School

I can see my dog outside wanting to come in
Pushing with all his might,
My mum on the computer
And my sister looking down over the banister,
I can hear the piano as the notes float through the air,
I can hear my dog barking and when he comes in
I hear scratching and hissing from my cats,
My mum on the computer, pitter-patter, pitter-patter,
I can taste some fizzy Skips burning on my tongue,
A chocolate biscuit coming into my mouth,
My mum's lovely dinner.

I can touch my cats' fur as they purr,
My dog's rough paws as he jumps up on me,
My mum's soft hands as she hugs me,
I can touch my dad's suit as he hugs me too,
I can smell my cats' food and mine,
My mum's lovely perfume soaking into her beautiful skin,
I can taste my mum's perfume because it is so strong,
Even though it is very noisy - I love my house!

Rachel Lines (9)
Hatfield Heath CP School

Home From School

I can see . . .
My mum changing the smelly baby's nappy,
I can see my sister lying on the sofa watching TV,
I can notice my mum cooking an extremely good tea,
I can see my very dirty dad coming in from work to help her.

I can hear . . .
My dog's heavy breathing,
I am listening to the noisy baby crying,
I can hear the boiling water bubbling on the Aga.

I can feel . . .
The baby's nice warm clothes,
I can touch the smooth oak dinner table,
I can touch the big blue beany bag.

I can smell . . .
My baby brother's smelly nappies,
I can sniff my mum's lovely cooking,
I can smell the healthy bananas and oranges.

I can taste . . .
The cool fresh water from the fridge.

George Wadhams (9)
Hatfield Heath CP School

Home From School

I can make out my brothers beating each other up,
Punching and kicking!
I can spot my mum making a delicious tea,
I can view myself in the mirror at the other end of the hall,
I can't believe it's me.

I can catch the telly on full blast,
I can listen to my brother's scream,
I can pick up the sound of bubbles in the pan,
While my mum is making tea.

I can taste the flavours my mum is cooking,
Can taste a mouthful of the crisps from my lunch box,
As salty as can be,
I can nibble the lolly from my friend,
As nice as can be.

I can scent the smell of polish
On the pine wood,
I can whiff the petrol from the cars
That has wafted in.

I can feel the soft comfortable sofa,
I can sit on it,
I can touch the remote and watch TV.

Zoe Wearden (8)
Hatfield Heath CP School

Home From School

I get to the front of the house,
I stand in the chilly street and ring the bell,
There is my mum.

When I get in the warm house,
My brother is screaming about a mouse,
My sister is watching TV loud,
My dad is cooking lamb and boiled potatoes.

I'm drinking sweet orange juice,
Which is lovely,
I taste the lamb and potatoes for my tea
And the apple pie, which comes for pudding.

The smelly leftover tea
And the juicy orange juice in my cup,
The apple pie still in my mouth.

Alexander Cleaves (9)
Hatfield Heath CP School

Winter Outside

The soft snow glitters,
The sun shines happily,
The birds sing,
Snow on the hills,
Bare trees,
The sky is blue,
Green confetti sways slowly,
The snow melts.

Shane Greenway (8)
Henham And Ugley Primary School

Evacuation

I stand here silent, I'm all alone
No more Dad
No more Mum

I stand here silent, I'm all alone
No more brothers
No more sisters

I stand here silent, I'm all alone
I feel so empty
Now everything's gone

I stand here silent, I'm all alone
No more noise
No more bickering

I stand here silent, I'm all alone
No more friends
No more home.

Lily Gould (11)
Henham And Ugley Primary School

A Snowy Day

It tastes like ice cream in a bowl with cream,
It looks like everything is under a spell in the field,
It sounds like children are shouting with joy in the playground,
It sounds like happiness is coming my way,
It makes me feel glad inside my heart,
It is whizzing all around me.

Holly Stewart (8)
Henham And Ugley Primary School

Where Is My Food?

I want more food, Mum
Mum, more food
I'll eat anything
Even if it's stewed!

Is rationing
Something we have to do?
I'll eat last week's leftovers
Anything I can chew

Please, please
Mum, please
I need more food
Even dry, mouldy cheese

Maybe some bread
Or some pork
I'm not picky
Anything to go on my fork

My stomach is rumbling
Food is my passion
Why, oh why
Do we have to ration?

Hayley Carter (11)
Henham And Ugley Primary School

A Snowy Day

Clear blue sky,
Snow falling from the trees,
Children laughing in the breeze,
Dazzling prints in the snow,
Sun shining, birds flying,
Smelling the fresh air.

Phoebe Kavanagh (8)
Henham And Ugley Primary School

I Hate Rationing

Every week I hear Mum say
I'm off to get the milk today

I hate rationing
I love food
I wish for chocolate
Not old stew

Mum likes cooking
Mum likes clothes
But why is it
That she always moans?

Dad likes chips
Dad likes fish
But he never
Gets a full dish

Every week I hear Mum say
I'm off to get the milk today

How I hate rationing!

Jeannie Mott Philip (10)
Henham And Ugley Primary School

I Love Chocolate

I love chocolate in the day and in the night
I love chocolate in the rain and in the sun
I love chocolate in the countryside and city
I love chocolate in the classroom and at home
But most of all I love chocolate in my . . .
Mouth!

Jessica Hogg (9)
Henham And Ugley Primary School

From Morning 'Til Night

The sun rises in the morning mist,
Dewdrops shimmer on flower heads.
Fluffy clouds glide across the sky,
Blackbirds sing and cockerels crow
As the countryside comes to life
And then the weather changes in a twist.

The wind begins to howl like a ghost in a haunted house,
Then rain starts to fall like diamonds dropping from the sky,
The drops get bigger and puddles form,
The rain lashes down, so children cry,
Claps of thunder make children scream,
As lightning zigzags across the sky
And looks like wax scrawled onto black sugarpaper.

Clouds disappear and the sky turns white,
Snowflakes start to fall,
Feathery ice crystals glisten on a fence
And children watch as snow mounds form,
Children laugh with delight
And then they have a snowball fight,
Snowballs whizz through the air,
A snowman is made of snow and ice
And later ice crystals start to dangle from his carrot nose.

The night draws in as dusk forms,
The sky turns black,
Stars twinkle in the night sky as the moon starts to glow,
The eerie darkness spreads all around,
Owls hoot in the trees and hedgehogs scuttle around looking for food,
Bats hang upside down between the branches
And in the garden you can see,
Frosty the snowman gleaming in the darkness,
Icicles start to fall from him,
As he slowly begins to melt!

Kirstie Dunbar (10)
Henham And Ugley Primary School

Haunted House

At the edge of the forest
Was a dark, dark house
Everyone that went in
Never came *out!*

I went in that house
The floorboards creaked
I screamed
I was totally freaked

An owl hooted
A ghost moaned
A witch cackled
They were coming to get me
Argh!

Eloise Robinson (9)
Henham And Ugley Primary School

Football

F ootball is a great sport
O f course you get muddy
O f course you have fun
T here are lots of fantastic players
B eckham is the best
A nd so is Zidane
L ots of people enjoy it
L ife is not complete without a ball at your feet.

Cameron Brown (10)
Henham And Ugley Primary School

But Seriously

B ut seriously why do you have to go
U sing all those guns out in the snow?
T rouble is so very near

S o why don't you just come stay here?
E rase the memory of war
R ight now don't go and obey the law
I don't want it to end this way
O h just come and stay one more day
U se my trust to get some glory
S tay, don't make it the end of the story
L et me not be reduced to tears
Y earning, anxious, full of fears.

Sam Hutchin (10)
Henham And Ugley Primary School

Swimming

S wim, swim, swim,
'W hat length can you swim?'
'I can swim 500m'
'M arvellous!'
M y mum says
I am the best swimmer she knows
'N o way, my
G randad's better than you!'

Sophie Cartledge (9)
Henham And Ugley Primary School

Rain

Rain comes down *fast* and *slowly*
Some rain goes pitter-patter, pitter-patter
And some rain goes plop, plop, plop
They form puddles, some *big* and some *small*
Some rain is *loud* and some rain is quiet
Some hang onto branches and some goes *straight* to the ground
Some rain goes *slush* by mixing with mud and some rain stays itself
By morning some rain is still there and some rain is gone.

Natasha Drake (9)
Henham And Ugley Primary School

Blackout

One night I drove my car,
But I didn't get very far,
Because I hit a sow,
Painted white like a cow,
It was near the local farm
And when I hit it, I said, 'Darn!'

Eleanor Griffiths (10)
Henham And Ugley Primary School

Revolting Things

Pirates puke on stormy seas,
Queens get stuck on top of trees,
Kings feel sick in golden loos,
Dogs throw up on daddies' shoes,
Babies love to make a mess
Down Mum's favourite dress
And this rhyme wouldn't be complete
Without the stench of last night's treat.

Eliott Simpson (7)
Manuden CP School

Shipwreck Song

A thousand foamy waves washed over the shipwreck,
Great anchors from a battle fleet scattered in the sand,
Skulls with glowing eyes,
No, not eyes but gems, mocking the eyes of men lay near
And in the midst of all this plunder,
Lying at the bottom of the briny sea
Lay -
A mask
Dolphins' sleek bodies shimmer from the exquisite pearls
patterned on it
The cool silver turned the shells to diamond
Bones to coral
The shipwreck was gone.

Emma Warbrick (10)
Manuden CP School

Once Upon A Rhyme . . .

Once upon a rhyme
In an ancient, mystic time
A creature lay in a cave
A monster lurked beneath the wave
A fair princess screamed from her mighty tower
A dark magician spread his power
A deadly potion bubbled and boiled
The handsome prince's plot was foiled
A knight's forgotten rusty sword
A deathly dragon's sparkling hoard . . .
Once upon a rhyme
In an ancient, mystic time . . .

Emma Simpson (11)
Manuden CP School

The Princess And The Pea

The prince was getting angry
He did not have a wife
And then he asked his mother
What would happen in his life
His mother said to get the maid
Who wouldn't come unless she's paid
Mother said, 'Of course she can
Just hurry up,' and down she ran
'Now get 19 mattresses and a pea
Then tuck it under for none to see'
Plans were made to meet some girls
They all arrived with hair in curls
All too soon night-time came
Then the morning all in shame
This happened for a thousand times
Each evening ending with the chimes
Until one cold and stormy night
A lady came all dressed in white
'I've lost my way
Please may I stay?'
'Yes . . . upstairs on your right
Hope you have a peaceful night'
Mother asked about her sleep
Then the girl began to weep
I felt a stone in there with me
Mother raised her hands in glee
Well here you are my handsome son
Let the wedding preparations be begun
And so they lived in bliss together
Happily forever and ever.

Emily Curtis (9)
Manuden CP School

What A Racket

Cats miaow
Dogs bark
Owls hoot
They like the dark
Turkeys gobble
Hens cluck
Pigs oink
They roll in the muck
Cows moo
Horses neigh
I think that's enough noise for the rest of the day!

Francesca Gee (9)
Manuden CP School

The Great Bald Eagle

The eagle flies so high
Gracefully in the sky
It swoops down to catch its prey
Injects its claws and eats that day.

Nicholas Davies (10)
Manuden CP School

The Aliens

The aliens fly in their saucers
Day and night they take over the world
Dropping bombs and deadly gasses
Killing all humans
Now the Earth is dead.

Danielle Gipps (8)
Manuden CP School

A Silly Argument

I heard a silly argument at the prince's house
'He'll choose me, I'm as silent as a mouse'
Cinderella put her hands over her ears and sang a silly tune
Snow White came in and blamed it on the moon
'You can't do that,' Sleeping Beauty yelled
It all got out of hand and someone said she smelled!
Then Rapunzel came in
And the prince came through
He went over to Rapunzel and said, 'I'll marry you.'

Bethany Walker (10)
Manuden CP School

Birthdays

B irthdays . . .
I love birthdays,
R ipping open presents,
T hen playing non-stop,
H aving a super time,
D ancing with joy,
A s hours pass by,
Y our presents scattered around,
S oon the day's over.

Nicole Gipps (10)
Manuden CP School

The Trees Are Blowing

The trees are blowing calmly
While the leaves are falling from the sky slowly as can be
While the children are trying to catch the leaves
When they fall from the sky
Then the wind blows harder and harder
It started blowing harder and harder
The next day the wind was not there.

George Fisher (9)
Manuden CP School

The Writer Of This Poem

(Based on 'The Writer Of This Poem' by Roger McGough)

The writer of this poem . . .
Is as soft as a kitten,
As strong as a giant,
As tall as a tree,
As pretty as a kitten,
As clever as a clown,
As loud as a trumpet,
As cute as a cat,
As sharp as a pencil
And as quick as a waiter.

Chloe Kemp (9)
Markyate Village School

Colours

As yellow as the midday sun
As green as grass
Black as can be
Grey as stormy days
Orange as sunset
Red like roses
Blue as chills in winter
Silver like icicles
Colours are precious things.

Charlotte Brown (9)
Markyate Village School

The Writer Of This Poem

(Based on 'The Writer Of This Poem' by Roger McGough)

The writer of this poem . . .
Is as quick as a leopard
As big as a giant
As funny as a clown
As pretty as a goddess
As good as gold
As well-dressed as a beautiful princess
As gentle as a rabbit
As strong as a volcano
As slim as a tree
As well make-upped as a goddess
As red as lips
As hard as stone
As busy as a bee
As clever as a brain
As bright as the sun.

Georgia Dear (8)
Markyate Village School

The Writer Of This Poem

(Based on 'The Writer Of This Poem' by Roger McGough)

The writer of this poem . . .
Is as beautiful as the glittering snowflakes
As gentle as a soft pillow
As pretty as a princess
As quiet as a goldfish
As cheeky as a monkey
As careful as a gold and glittery star
As red as a rose.

Elle Burchmore (8)
Markyate Village School

The Writer Of This Poem

(Based on 'The Writer Of This Poem' by Roger McGough)

The writer of this poem . . .
Is as tall as can be
As funny as a clown
As unique as a key

As clever as a fox
As bouncy as a ball
As strong as steel
As loud as a call

As lively as a cheetah
As weird as a rat
As wobbly as jelly
As silent as a bat

The writer of this poem
Is everything you see
The writer of this poem
Is me.

Jessica Perks (9)
Markyate Village School

The Feet

At night the feet became lonely
All day they are important
Squashed in shoes and socks
While you are playing
Kicking in the water when you swim around
But at night they feel tired and hot
They sweat and smell
All they want to do is sleep.

Anna Hickson (8)
Markyate Village School

Laura Max

Laura Max was as ugly as a pear
Everybody hated her ugly hair
The one thing that was horrible about Laura Max
Was she always ate her ugly earwax
One day Laura Max
Had all earwax
Over her ugly face
She said she was going on holiday with a suitcase
She picked her brain out, she was at the airport
Hadn't had a thought
Her brain was so small
The next day she was caught at the mall
She exploded so she was really small.

Tom Sharp (8)
Markyate Village School

The Writer Of This Poem

(Based on 'The Writer Of This Poem' by Roger McGough)

The writer of this poem . . .
Is as quick as a flea
As strong as iron
As great as a king
As clever as a brain
As good as gold
As bold as a giant
The writer of this poem
Is greater than everything!

David Smith (9)
Markyate Village School

Similes

As fluffy as a poodle!
As red as fire!
As red as anger!
As hot as lava!
As smelly as a bin!
As yellow as the sun!
As purple as an octopus!
As fluffy as a kitten!
As dark as the sewers!
As brown as the old oak tree!
As white as snow!
As purple as a grape!
As magical as magic!
As cold as ice!

Megan Wilder-Harris (9)
Markyate Village School

Tom Pose

Tom Pose was a chubby lad,
He was incredibly mad,
Everybody hated him
But he was good at gym,
They hated him because he picked his nose
And he had such ugly toes.

One day he picked too deep
And it made him leap,
He pulled out his brain,
The doctors chucked it down the drain,
Then one day he was seen exploding,
While he was loading.

Laura McKenna (9)
Markyate Village School

Colours

Green as nature's life,
Red as lava,
Blue as chills in winter,
Purple as dark nights and storms,
White as fluffy clouds,
Yellow as the noonday sun,
Pink as flowers growing,
Black as black can be,
Golden as the sun,
Orange as a sunset,
Grey as a stormy day . . .
But all the colours are great!

Emily Upson (8)
Markyate Village School

Deedee

This is the tale of Speedy Deedee
Who's really greedy
She ate too much
And spoke some Dutch
And then felt really ill
But still at will
And yet she ate
Until it was late
Until she blew up.

Jody Onyett (9)
Markyate Village School

Picking Nose

Mr Spear went out to play
When he came back, he fell in clay
He went to hospital in a hurry
And while he was there he ate some curry
The doctors could do their best
But the other doctors did the rest
But poor old Mr Spear picked his nose
And went back to hospital on his toes
Poor old Mr Spear went on a bed
And had another dread
And in the morning he was dead.

Lewis Baldwin (8)
Markyate Village School

Mr Chumb

Oh you want to know a story about a boy called Mr Chumb
He was a funny old lad but he sucked his thumb
'Where's my thumb?' cried Mr Chumb
'Oh Mum, you're a chumb,' screeched Mr Chumb
Mrs Chumb went away just that day
Mr Chumb was wasting away.

Melissa Bate (8)
Markyate Village School

The Seashore

The waves roll and whirl above your head
Your feet lay calmly on the soft seabed
Above, the sun shines, bright and bold
The children playing on the sand, so gold

Silvery fishes in the bright blue sea
Quietly swim away from me
But the children on the smooth, silky sand
Come crashing in the sea like a great brass band

On the sand, so big and grand
Towns of golden castles stand
But in the exotic wavy sea
Everyone's as noisy as can be!

Abigail Robbins (10)
Northgate Primary School

Simon The Lion

Simon the lion has a mane like fire,
He's got a tail the ladies desire.

Simon the lion's got robust legs,
He's also got teeth like camping pegs!

Simon the lion's got a sopping wet nose,
He's got teeth to bite off toes!

Simon the lion's got eyes like stone,
He parades over the African plains alone.

Ben Bull (11)
Northgate Primary School

Autumn

I stood under an old oak tree
And gazed at the leaves surrounding me,
Crimsons, golds and newly fallen greens
Are brushed into piles as the park-keeper cleans.
As the leaves fly round about,
The little children scream and shout,
In the mass of crunchy leaves
That have tumbled from the trees!
A ghostly shape falls upon the ground,
A skeleton leaf, detailed golden-brown,
I pick it up between gentle fingers,
The scent of autumn faraway lingers.
I look a the patterns of the crumpled shape,
Thinking how many replicas trees have to make,
For this leaf that is cold and dead,
Has lived its life, turning green to red,
As tops of the trees and the churches it passed,
As I released it from my grasp,
I let my pretty leaf go
And let it float slowly over treetops below.

Amy Goldsworthy (11)
Northgate Primary School

Candlelight

Mellow light swaying from side to side,
Blown by the drought from the window and blind.

Burning wax flowing in a stream,
Changed from the solid it used to be.

You're used to celebrate on special occasion,
Your flame brings happiness and relaxation.

Your slow and dozy movements calm down a busy day,
You can stand straight and proud, or droop like a dead flower.

You will be used for the rest of time,
By animal and human alike.

Jack Rowbottom (11)
Northgate Primary School

Candlelight

A candle with a physique shape,
A wick that burns with a thousand flames.

Angelic and beautiful, slender and elegant,
The candle is peace and tranquillity at its best.

It can also bring sorrow, death and mourning,
A candle lights the way for travellers at night.

The flame is hypnotic,
Like a siren's song.

A candle is comfort and relaxation,
Candles are sanctuary, welcome and warm.

Flickering and dancing, cascading shadows,
Candles glow with a glint of an eye.

Eleanor Treadwell (11)
Northgate Primary School

My Parrot

Eyes like black beads of bracelet,
A voice like a choir that sings.
She wears a patchwork feather quilt
And still has room for her wings!

Her beak is like Captain Hook's cutlass
Curved, pointed and long.
Her feet are like Blu-Tack on paper,
Sticking to the branch that they're on!

Her feathers are as soft as a feather quilt,
She has claws as sharp as nails
And every night for her dinner,
I feed her a whole bag of snails!

Alice Menhennet (11)
Northgate Primary School

A Storm On A Rocky Cliff

Far away in the Isle of Wight,
Three ships were sailing when they had a big fright,
The ships started tossing, (it was just after sunset),
When all of a sudden the ships came and met.

They crashed together, tossing men overboard,
The crew started struggling getting out the oars,
Then all of a sudden the ships started sinking,
Then old Bill the cabin boy really started thinking.

'We might have to swim for it, dive in and splash!'
So all of them did so and then they watched the ships crash!
They were lucky they got away, they swam very fast,
They saw the sun shining down and they saw the clouds fly past.

They climbed onto some massive rocks and climbed up to the peak,
The rocks were very confusing so they decided to play hide-and-seek.
One of the men found a castle, most of it was knocked down,
He walked around and he really liked it, so he didn't make a frown.

The other men found the castle and went inside as well,
They found the other man and corridors and four cells.
They lit a big fire and all danced around, glad that they were steady,
The town in the distance saw the fire and got the rescue plane ready.

The pilot flew closer and landed on the top,
The pilot got out, found the men and in they all did hop.
They all flew glad and safe, back to their own town,
They said thank you to the rescue man and then they all got down!

Ella Dolding (9)
Northgate Primary School

Black

Black is the colour of a jet flying in the lit sky,
The colour of a lucky black cat
And the colour of night, riding a horse.
Black is the colour of death on the ground, against a wall
And of a shadow, flat on the ground.
Black is the colour of a crow flying
And of soot in the fireplace.
Black is the colour of loneliness all around,
The darkness of boredom, of a fright at night.
Black is the colour of guilt and disappointment,
The colour of a never-ending tunnel, big and dark
And the colour of a sinister deep hole,
Black is the colour of sadness in your dreams.

Rebecca Coltart (11)
Northgate Primary School

The Seashore

There is a village by the sea
And little boys and girls looking out at the sea
In my house I am alone getting my boat
I better get out there or the tide will come in
And there will be too much sea!
Here I am in the sea and I'm underwater
And so is my beautiful oldest daughter
I enjoy going out to sea
And the beautiful lights of the town I see!

Charlotte Doyle (9)
Northgate Primary School

Seascape

Down by the sea
Was where I used to be
And in the bay
Where I used to play
There, something lay

A little fishing boat
Around a little moat
And in it I used to sit
Rocking it a little bit

The next day
I went to the bay
I had a big surprise
For there on the sunrise

I saw my little ship
And as I took a sip
From my drink
It danced like it was on an ice rink.

Robert Davis (9)
Northgate Primary School

Down By The Station

Lots of people in the station
Trains going *choo-choo* chuffing all day long
Lots of smoke going all over the station
People waiting for trains on the platforms
Windows steaming up from all the smoke
People coughing full of smoke
Lots of buildings in the background
Lots of flowers blooming full of colour.

Hayley Shaw (9)
Northgate Primary School

Weird

Poor old Sophie she had a big fright
When she saw an alien in the middle of the night.
'Argh!' she screamed, 'go away!'
But the alien just wanted to stay.

The alien said, 'Blah bloggie boo gloo!'
But Sophie just screamed, 'Oh boohoo!
Just go away, I don't want you here!'
But the alien said, 'Oh dear, oh dear!'

Sophie understood him, she really did!
She jumped up and down but the alien hid.
Sophie said, 'I understand you I really do!'
The alien jumped up and said, 'Whoopee for you!

My spaceship has crashed, please help me do.'
'Oh well, that's unlucky for you.
I'll give it a go, I can't promise anything.'
'Oh it will be better than nothing.'

Sophie gave it a go and it worked out all fine,
The alien lifted off and said, 'This ship is divine!'
'Thank you,' said Sophie, 'come back again.
Oh and next time come and see my brother, Ben.'

Lauren Nelson (9)
Northgate Primary School

Tree

Weeping sad and lonely tears,
Growing, growing through the years.
Leaves are gained when spring arrives,
When they have fallen, autumn's alive.

Giving us oxygen through the year,
Sleeping, sleeping, winter's here.
Every day the roots get stronger,
Branches are getting longer and longer.

Alena Bigg (10)
Northgate Primary School

The Boat Memory

I went on a boat out to sea
With only the oarsman, my baby and me
I miss my husband and my teenage son
But our boating adventure has scarcely begun

We soon got hungry my baby and I
We looked at the oarsman, he had lost his left eye!
I stopped for a moment, I was not that keen
But my little baby gave out a loud scream

'I lost this eye in a war,' he said
But a week before it was bloody and red
I fought in the war with McCallum McCault
We both shot a gun in the war that we fought'

'Get me off this boat now, before I jump'
Said the lady who'd whined and looked like a grump
'Don't worry my dear, I'm not really here
It's only a dream, I'm sailing up here . . .'

Ben Stauber (9)
Northgate Primary School

The New Chef

Spaghetti Bolognese tastes wonderfully nice
So does calamari, with hot sweetcorn and rice
Fish and shrimps and prawns go into the stew
The garlic bread's so chunky you have to chew and chew!

A man in tattered clothes walks through the polished door
'Mmm, that smells so good!' he said.
'Shame I am so poor!'

'Come on in and work with us!' we shouted at the guy
He cooked with us for many years
'Til time came for him to die.

Tabitha Tingey (9)
Northgate Primary School

The Cancan

Far away in France on a stage doing a dance
Kicking their legs, holding their dress
This dance is called the cancan

Far away in France on a stage doing a dance
Audience cheering, people are singing
This dance is called the cancan

Far away in France on a stage doing a dance
Ladies in red dresses, men in big laces
This dance is called the cancan

Far away in France on a stage doing a dance
People are smiling, people are dining
This dance is called the cancan.

Ben Springham (9)
Northgate Primary School

Sally The Spider

Sally the spider was most at home
Sitting slyly by the telephone
Sally was always extraordinarily scary
But all the time watching out and wary

Sitting in her web one wonderful day
Sally saw a fly come out to play
She was there as quick as a cheetah
She gobbled it down as quick as you can say heater

Snaking along came a human that night
Sally gave him a great big fright
In fact there was a squat to make her pay
And just to get Sally out of the way.

Peter Connell (10)
Northgate Primary School

The Festival Of Light

Today we celebrate electricity
The celebration is in Italy
So today we celebrate electricity
It makes our surroundings bright

Tonight we start to sing and dance
And tired people go into a trance
So come on, let's get ready
But get ready nice and steady

Come on, get in the car
Because Italy is quite far
Now that we are here
There's nothing more to fear

Our surroundings are very bright
It is a marvellous sight
Oh look at the orchestra play
And the choir are also having their say

Oh no, we have to go home
And go home to the nice and cosy bed
Oh well it has been a brilliant day
And good for fun and play.

Samuel Kightley (9)
Northgate Primary School

High In The Sky

Vishnu and Lakshmi riding on Garuda in the sky,
Getting closer to home, where they can say goodbye.
Speeding up through the air,
With rushing wind through their hair.

They zoom down and catch some squid
And put it in a jar with a lid
A storm brewed up over there
But they got away with the wind in their hair

Getting closer to home
It looks like a really big dome
With its glittering spark
It looks horrible when it's dark

Now they're here and Garuda flew off
They feel so sad and went to jump off
They felt so sad because of leaving Garuda
So they sat down and ate some barracuda.

Bradley Stevens (9)
Northgate Primary School

The Underground

My dad comes home on a train, on a train called the underground,
He comes home with Simon, Phil, Sarah, Freddy and Mr Hound,
People in suits with black bow ties, black high heels and cuffs,
When my dad gets home because it is hot, he had lots of
huffs and puffs.

One day I went to work with my dad,
But coming home I never knew it would be so bad.
Coming home on the train,
I never knew it would be so puffy and stuffy.

Now I will never go on that train again!

Katherine Terris (9)
Northgate Primary School

The Big Banquet

On the edge of an island, next to the sea,
Come along now, follow me.
Join the people, join the fun,
Make this time jolly for everyone.

Coloured flowers, purple and green
And a tasty banquet fit for the queen.
Coloured bushes, blue and red,
'We feel so happy,' the children said.

All the adults drinking fine wine,
Exclaimed so loudly, 'This wine is divine!'
Laughter is heard for miles around,
It makes a fabulous jolly old sound.

On the edge of an island, next to the sea,
Come along now, follow me.

Lucy Menzies (9)
Northgate Primary School

The Seaside

There is a village by the sea,
With people passing by,
The coconuts falling from the trees,
Then people go and collect them,
You see the seagulls flying through the air,
All the day you hear the swish-swash of the sea hitting the seashore.

Lia Woodward (9)
Northgate Primary School

Colonel Fazackerley

(Inspired by 'Colonel Fazackerley' by Charles Causley)

Colonel Fazackerley Butterworth-Toast
Bought an old castle complete with a ghost
But someone or other forget to declare
To Colonel Fazack that the spectre was there

On the very first evening, while waiting to dine
The Colonel was taking a fine sherry wine
When the ghost, with a furious flash and a flare
Shot out of the chimney and shivered, 'Beware!'

Colonel Fazackerley Butterworth-Toast,
Was a bit annoyed with this gloomy old ghost,
So he reached for the Hoover and flicked on the switch
And threw out the Hoover into a ditch.

From this day on the ghost is still there
And he's now getting old with strands of grey hair.
The ghost has retired, he now likes to knit,
He's ever so glad he decided to quit!

As for Colonel Fazackerley, another story to tell,
Let's just say he is not at all well.
He's got a disease, it's really quite bad,
He's missing the ghost he once never had.

Lucy Crossfield (10)
Northgate Primary School

A Magical Place To Be

Sea wishing washing, gently across the bay,
Seagulls swooping downwards, searching for their prey,
The sea is so colourful, like a shining star,
The sea is so beautiful, with fish from afar.

The sea is a lovely place to be,
Where children like to play, just like you and me,
The fishing boats come crowding in,
The beautiful fish, all pulled in.

The sandcastles are all knocked over,
The children all go home,
When the crowds are gone,
The beach is no more than the sea.

The white puffy clouds up in the deep blue sky,
Birds flying south, crying their goodbyes,
Out and beyond in the distance, glistening far away,
How I love to watch the sunset, on the seashore's bay.

Krystina Sumner (9)
Northgate Primary School

Sammy The Spider

Sammy spider scuttles in the dark,
Sammy's found under big bark.
But Sammy has a tale of woe,
About someone's big old toe!

One hot summer's day,
Sammy saw someone play.
So scuttle as he might,
He had one big *fright!*

The human's big toe
Got stuck down his hole!
So Sammy fetched one big pole
And poked out the toe.

When Sammy went out,
He made a big pout
'Cause someone picked up Sammy
And made him all jammy.

Christian Dalton (9)
Northgate Primary School

A Rap

Once I was bored, so I got up and said,
'Yo, yo, everybody, I'm gonna rap round your head.'
I rapped right here, I rapped right there,
In fact I rapped everywhere.
My dad looked amazed, my mum looked scared
And my angry little sis just stood up and glared.
Then I rapped out the door and down to the park,
Where it was getting really dark.
I rapped right here, I rapped right there,
In fact I rapped everywhere.
Jack looked amazed, Guy looked scared
And Joe got angry then stood up and glared.
But it was time to go home, to go to bed,
Then I thought, *tomorrow I'll rap round their heads.*

Ciaran Daly (9)
Roundwood Primary School

Can We Get A Hamster?

'Can we get a hamster, Mum?'
'No, two goldfish are enough.'
'Come on Mum, do you honestly think
That caring for goldfish is tough?'

'Can we get a hamster, Dad?'
'No, they always escape.'
'Come on Dad, if we just get a hamster,
I'll secure the cage with tape!'

'Can we get a hamster, Gran?'
'No, they smell unpleasant.'
'Come on Gran, I'd clean him out,
I'm not a little infant!'

'Can we get a hamster, Luke?'
'Yeah sure, let's go.'
So now we've got a hamster,
Thanks to my big bro!

Tamsin Asquith (8)
Roundwood Primary School

The Weather

The happy bride stands silent and still,
A frosty veil covering her face,
Her outstretched arms, branches.

A cold, white blanket covers the ground,
Snowflakes falling like little puffs of white smoke,
Adding to the vast stretch of coldness.

Dappled sunlight, spreading like a fiery angel
Over the world,
Peeking through the curtains to wake you.

Crystals shower down from Heaven,
Sparkling like the sun on the sea,
Creating puddles of diamonds.

Ione Woods (9)
Roundwood Primary School

Sara-Jane

Sara-Jane is very strange,
She keeps a red and blue bird box
In her domain,
You funny Sara-Jane.

Sara-Jane is very weird,
She had to make sure
Her good reputation is to be cleared,
You're funny Sara-Jane.

Sara-Jane is very crazy,
When it was cold,
She said it was hazy,
You're funny Sara-Jane.

Sara-Jane is my best friend
And good friends are we,
We shall be friends until the end,
That Sara-Jane and me!

Robin Smith (8)
Roundwood Primary School

Recipe For A Dragon

Take a head as round as a marble,
A body as thick as trees
And spikes as sharp as swords.

Add scales as precious as rubies,
Wings as strong as metal
And a tail as long as a whip.

Decorate with eyes like glinting diamonds,
Teeth as white as angels
And claws as long as canes.

Stir in a fiery mixture as hot as fire itself,
And bake for 1,000 years
And you have made a dragon.
Beware!

Rowan Lawton (9)
Roundwood Primary School

The Tiger

Tiger, on your sand-strewn island,
As yellow as the bright morning sun,
You are, tiger, the golden crown.
Butter hue, sharp, white claws,
Most muscular are your movements,
Handsome you are in your youth.
God has granted you for life,
Lordship of the green, grassy jungle.

Two skills keep you from hunting,
Splendid gifts granted to you.
You are a master killer,
Look at your tactics on the mountains
And you are able to jump,
Far above the cut down trees,
Staring down, a fearsome beast,
To survey the land's surface.
Scanning the ground below,
Harvesting jungle deer like ripe oranges.
You run the lands superbly,
To waylay prey from escaping.
Your fur, fair creature,
Is your rough and lovely tail,
Keeper of the ferocious jungle,
Breast the colour of shining gold money,
You gleam in the high rocky mountains.

In a sand-strewn shirt,
A doublet, thousand stars,
With a bright moon for a gown,
You are a beast among animals,
Yellow cloaked, a stampede of the jungle.

Alice Gosling (8)
Roundwood Primary School

Pets

My horse is brown like a chocolate bar,
Swishing his midnight mane,
Galloping like the cold wind.

My dog is gold like the sun in the sky,
Chasing mice and rabbits,
Running madly round the garden.

My rabbit is white like the sparkling snow,
Munching food all day long,
Hopping over the grass.

My cat is black like the soot in the chimney,
Strolling over the path,
Never ever getting lost.

Cristina McNabola (9)
Roundwood Primary School

The Tiger

Take a head as round as a World Cup football,
Decorate with orange and black stripes,
Golden eyes staring at its prey,
Add a tail swinging from side to side,
Take four fangs and stick them
On the top and bottom of its mouth,
Stir and boil for twelve hours.

Beware! You have a tiger.

Elliot Jones (8)
Roundwood Primary School

The Lion

Lion, on the dry desert,
As golden as the mid-morning sun,
You are, big cat, the king of beasts,
Shining hue, pad-footed,
Beautiful you are, throughout your life.

Two skills keep you away from your deathbed,
Exquisite gifts, given to you.
You run amazingly fast,
You sprint from danger excellently.
Look at your skill alone on the African plains
And you are able to hunt
Any animal you like.
Your teeth are your killers,
As sharp as daggers.

Breast the colour of melted butter,
In a bronze-coloured coat.
You stand out on the dull land surrounding you.
You are, lion, an animal of complete brilliance.

Caitlin Scholey (8)
Roundwood Primary School

Plains Of Africa

Covered like savannah, the plains rest.
Gazelles jumping happily, the plains rest.
Predators pouncing cautiously, the plains rest.
Trees swaying in the wind, the plains rest.
Birds flying in the wind, the plains rest.
Men hunting animals, the plains rest.
Night coming like lightning, animals sleep.
Everything silent, the plains awake!

Simon Williams (8)
Roundwood Primary School

The Sun

The sun is shining in the golden summer sky,
Turning your frowns upside down.
Children have water fights, squealing, running around.

Snow:
Fluffy cotton wool drifting down like a blanket being spread out,
Snow angels appear suddenly and snowballs greet you in the face.

Frost:
The branches sparkle as the weak sunlight peeks through the clouds,
The birds sing to wake you to see this lovely sight.

Fog:
The fog is like smoke blocking the path,
You look ahead, but see nothing but a grey trail,
Like a dream, but real.

Sarah Graham (9)
Roundwood Primary School

Snow

The snow is like a soft, white kitten
Falling swiftly in the air.

It is like a crunchy pack of leaves
Crackling in the breeze.

But sometimes it can be strong
It can go in your eyes
Like somebody biting your fingers off.

A blinding frost
A strong, white power
A road blocker
A car stealer
And a grass whitener.

Georgia Ledwidge (9)
Roundwood Primary School

What Is Green?

What is green?
A frog is green,
Swimming in the stream.

What is white?
The moon is white,
Floating like a kite.

What is red?
Mars is red,
Just like blood from your head.

What is brown?
My guinea pig is brown,
Squealing like a scared hound.

What is gold?
Gold is gold,
Just gold.

Harry Pattinson (8)
Roundwood Primary School

What is Grey And Slippery?

What is grey and slippery?
A grey and slippery fish on the tip of a dish
Is grey and slippery.

What is red and wet and big?
A big flood of red, wet blood
Is red, wet and big.

What is blue and small and salty and annoying?
A blue, small, salty and annoying flea
Is blue and small and salty and annoying.

What is yellow and hot and not very nice to eat and huge?
The yellow, hot, huge and not very nice to eat sun
Is yellow and hot and huge and not very nice to eat.

Joe Carr (9)
Roundwood Primary School

My Family

My mum is like a robot,
She can do eight things at once.

My dad is like a hippo,
He is the family dunce.

My sister's like a poodle,
She has to look her best.

My brother's like a beast,
He walks around undressed.

My nan is like a diary,
You can tell her all your fears.

My grandad's like a pig,
Loading up on beers.

And me?
Well, I'm just me, you see!

Tanya Emsley (9)
Roundwood Primary School

A Boy Named David

His hair is as baggy as a mop
Covering his ears and eyebrows.
His eyes seem to be closed at all times
And his nose is like a lump of clay.
His mouth is also as tiny as a raspberry.

His body is as skinny as a stone
And his legs are as dark as the pitch-black, gloomy night.
Also, his shoes are like suction boots,
Ready to walk on the wall.

Timothy McMillin (8)
Roundwood Primary School

My Friends And Family

My friend Polly
Is very, very jolly,
We always play around together
And play outside whatever the weather.

My cousin Joe
Likes to play down low,
We like to play planes
And play running up the lanes.

My weird mum
Lies quietly in the sun,
At weekends we go to the park,
When she meets her friend called Mark.

My clown dad
Is like a young lad,
He thinks he's like a super model,
But have you seen his silly waddle?

My sister Nicky
Always tries to kick me,
She gets on my nerves,
I can't find the right words.

So that's my family,
As you can see,
I'm glad I live with them though,
Because I do love them so.

Lauren Mitchell (9)
Roundwood Primary School

The Lion

Lion, on the plains of Africa,
As golden as the sun.
You are lion, the king of all big cats.
God has granted you for life,
Lordship of the African plains.
Two skills keep you from being killed.
Your fur is the colour of dripping butter
And you are able to catch your prey
Any time you feel hungry.
When you turn around,
You look like a fearsome beast.
You are a skilful hunter and killer,
You speed across the African plains
As fast as lightning.
You waylay buffalo from the stampede.
Sharp-toothed and most fearsome is your roar,
You are daylight hued.

George Fitzgerald (9)
Roundwood Primary School

My Family

My dad is like a monkey
As silly as can be
He isn't very funny
As you will always see.

My brother is like an aeroplane
Whizzing round the house
Breaking all the toys and games
He is not like a mouse.

My mum is like a Viking
As vicious as can be
A really violent person
Smashing everything she sees!
(Only kidding!)

Emma Peddle (9)
Roundwood Primary School

The Jaguar

Jaguar, in your dark, dense jungle,
As vivid blue as the dark, midnight sky,
You are, jaguar, lord of all beasts,
You are like the Prime Minister of England,
Your hue sapphire, black spotted.

Two skills keep you from perishing,
Great gifts given to you.
Your speed through the thicket
And you are a skilful hunter,
You cover the ground easily,
You waylay buffalo from the stampede,
You are a master at catching prey,
Your weapons are your teeth
And your strong, white claws.

You are keeper of the thick, dense jungle,
You roam across the jungle land,
In ink-coloured robes,
A beautiful cloak you possess,
You keep your family living,
You have great responsibility,
You are a wonderful animal.
Perfect though, you are not,
You look picturesque silhouetted against the moon,
You have a jacket of dark blue murky water,
Covered with black dashes.

Kieran Vaghela (8)
Roundwood Primary School

What Is Green?

What is green?
The grass is green
In the morning when it's clean.

What is blue?
Water is blue
When it's flushing down the loo.

What is brown?
A door is brown
When it's broken down.

What is grey?
A banana is grey
When it has been thrown away.

What is white?
A plane is white
In mid flight.

What is diamond?
A diamond is diamond,
Just diamond.

Harry Wells (8)
Roundwood Primary School

My Favourite Thing

My favourite thing
Is an eagle flapping its wings.
My favourite smell
Is the smell of baked beans in their tin.
My favourite sight
Is looking close-up on a candle light.
My favourite sound
Is the dropping of a pound (into my hand)!
My favourite taste
Is salmon fish paste.
These are a few of my favourite things.

David Phillips (8)
Roundwood Primary School

Fireworks

The Catherine wheel is like a dragon
Breathing green, dazzling fire.
A skull - white striped line firing to the moon.
The rocket spitting flames,
Bursting down faster than the eye can see.
The fountain sparklers brighter than the moonlight
And hotter than burning, red fire.
Fireworks spurting in the air, into different colours.

Oliver Wall (8)
Roundwood Primary School

Blue

Blue reminds me of the peaceful sea on holiday.
Blue reminds me of the lovely sky on sunny days.
Blue reminds me of raindrops falling on the windowpane.
Blue reminds me of bluebirds on a summer's day.
Blue reminds me of squishy blueberries and how they fall.
Blue reminds me of Tottenham Hotspur because my teacher
supports Tottenham.
Blue reminds me of waves on a calm sea.
Blue reminds me of my school uniform I wear five times a week.
Blue reminds me of peaceful music and how it sounds.
Blue reminds me of bluebells dancing in the wind.
Blue reminds me of big blue whales flapping their fins.
Blue reminds me of calm water tickling on my hands.
Blue reminds me of the colour and it's one of my favourites.

Georgie Fielden (8)
St Catherine's RC Primary School, Barnet

Blue

Blue reminds me of sea slushing against the waves.
Blue reminds me of bluebirds and their peaceful music.
Blue reminds me of the deep blue sea.
Blue reminds me of the summery blue sky.
Blue reminds me of a Catherine wheel spinning around.
Blue reminds me of raindrops dropping down.
Blue reminds me of blue, the colour that brightens up my day.
Blue reminds me of blueberries.
Blue reminds me of St Catherine's football kit.
Blue reminds me of Tottenham Hotspur winning a game.
Blue reminds me of bluebells ringing in the summer.

Lianne Steele (8)
St Catherine's RC Primary School, Barnet

Red

Red reminds me of a Red Nose Day at school.
Red reminds me of a red rose in a green field.
Red reminds me of a red ladybird fluttering in the sky.
Red reminds me of the fire brigade roaring down the road.
Red reminds me of red tomatoes hanging in my next-door
neighbour's greenhouse.
Red reminds me of red baubles hanging on a Christmas tree.
Red reminds me of the red-hot sun shining in the sky.

Charlotte Carey (8)
St Catherine's RC Primary School, Barnet

Yellow

Yellow reminds me of the beautiful, bright sun shining bright
on a beautiful summer's day.
Yellow reminds me of the daffodils waving in the summer breeze.
Yellow reminds me of the holidays on a beautiful day on the beach.
Yellow reminds me of the squashy banana in my school lunch box.
Yellow reminds me of the big, fierce lion pouncing around and
finding his food.
Yellow reminds me of watching the yellow sunflower growing
higher and higher.
Yellow reminds me of the little mouse munching on some cheese.
Yellow reminds me of pale yellow primroses waving on a high hill.
Yellow reminds me of shining buttercups sitting on a high mountain.

Rosie Curtis (8)
St Catherine's RC Primary School, Barnet

Blue

Blue reminds me of the deep blue sea when I went on holiday.
Blue reminds me of the blue waves when I am swimming in the sea.
Blue reminds me of the blue sky above me.
Blue reminds me of the wonderful bluebirds.
Blue reminds me of the water in the sea.
Blue reminds me of the blueberries when I eat them in the summer.
Blue reminds me of the raindrops falling from the sky.
Blue reminds me of a Catherine wheel.
Blue reminds me of the uniform that we wear at school.

Anastasia Elias (8)
St Catherine's RC Primary School, Barnet

Red

Red reminds me of Manchester United winning every game.
Red reminds me of the roses in my garden.
Red reminds me of the embarrassment I have been through.
Red reminds me of the red bike that I used to ride.
Red reminds me of the fire brigade that rides on the road where I live.
Red reminds me of my brother getting cross with me.
Red reminds me of Santa coming at night on Christmas Day.
Red reminds me of the blood running through our bodies.
Red reminds me of when my brother gets angry with me for not listening to him.
Red reminds me of Arsenal winning some games.
Red reminds me of a ladybird sitting on a leaf.
Red reminds me of the robin coming out at Christmas time.

James Dao (8)
St Catherine's RC Primary School, Barnet

Red

Red reminds me of Manchester United winning every match.
It also reminds me of big red roses in a field of green
And it always reminds me of molten metal when shaped into useful things.
Every day it reminds me of steelworks when they melt rocks for metal.
Red reminds me of ladybirds flying all around me.
Now I have to go away,
I will see you on another red-hot day.

David Ward (8)
St Catherine's RC Primary School, Barnet

Red

Red reminds me of the lovely roses that grow in the
summer sunshine.
Red reminds me of Manchester United winning every game.
Red reminds me of Santa Claus bringing presents to
everyone in the world.
Red reminds me of Valentine's Day and people giving cards.
Red reminds me of Red Nose Day which we raise money for.
Red reminds me of the red breasted robins sitting in the trees.
Red reminds me of the love hearts on Valentine's cards.
Red reminds me of the beautiful ladybirds sitting peacefully
on a leaf.
Red reminds me of the lipstick that my mum puts on her lips.
Red reminds me of my face when I get cross.
Red reminds me of the postbox that I send letters through.
Red reminds me of the firemen that save people's lives.
Red reminds me of the blood when I fall over.

Amy McGann (8)
St Catherine's RC Primary School, Barnet

Yellow

Yellow reminds me of Arsenal winning every match.
Yellow reminds me of the sand on the sunny beaches.
Yellow reminds me of the delicious pasta cooking in a saucepan.
Yellow reminds me of big, juicy melons.
Yellow reminds me of the corn growing in the green fields.
Yellow reminds me of buttercups shining brightly.
Yellow reminds me of the sunset shining everywhere.
Yellow reminds me of the bananas singing beautifully.

Ciaran Power (8)
St Catherine's RC Primary School, Barnet

Yellow

Yellow reminds me of the sun which is clear and bright.
It gives us all energy, it gives us all light.
Yellow reminds me of the sunflowers and the petals that gleam.
It looks like it's gone somewhere. I wonder where it's been?
Yellow reminds me of the sand and I see people's footsteps in it.
I hear people coming in just a bit.
Yellow reminds me of sweetcorn, small but sweet.
If I were you I'd think of eating it, I think it would be a treat.
Yellow reminds me of honey, sweet and sticky honey.
I know someone who would like it, I'd give it to a bunny.
Yellow reminds me of bananas, I'd make a banana split.
I'd train to be a baker, I'd train to be fit.

Claire Li (8)
St Catherine's RC Primary School, Barnet

Yellow

Beaches with sandcastles all around in Lanzarote, far, far away.
Pasta and sweetcorn on your plate, eat it up or it will be eaten by me!
Yellow lions roaring all the time, but watch out, they won't be far away.
Daffodils, buttercups in a green field, like a big, green blanket over the land.
Yellow reminds me of yellow, golden hair, swinging back and forth all the time.
Yellow reminds me of creamy cheese which little mice bite into.

Nicole Bradford (8)
St Catherine's RC Primary School, Barnet

Yellow

Yellow reminds me of the sun shining in my face very brightly.
Yellow reminds me of the gold butter in my fridge.
Yellow reminds me of the buttercups in the lovely green field
when it's hot.
Yellow reminds me of the pancakes with lemons on top.
Yellow reminds me of the ripe banana in my lunch box.
Yellow reminds me of the fresh cheese late at night.
Yellow reminds me of the daffodils when I'm walking home
from school.
Yellow reminds me of the pasta my mum cooks.
Yellow reminds me of the dandelions I see on Valentine's Day.
Yellow reminds me of the melons I see in the shops.
Yellow reminds me of the hot sand when I go on holiday.
Yellow reminds me of the lions I see at the zoo.
Yellow reminds me of very sticky honey.

Katherine Stainton (8)
St Catherine's RC Primary School, Barnet

Red

Red reminds me of Manchester United winning each game.
Red reminds me of embarrassment when my parents go red.
Red reminds me of red roses that you get on Valentine's Day
when you're in love.
Red reminds me of Arsenal who I absolutely *hate.*
Red reminds me of tomatoes that I eat in my salad.
Red reminds me of blood that keeps me alive.
Red reminds me of the Devil that I don't believe in.

Stacy Duru (8)
St Catherine's RC Primary School, Barnet

Blue

Blue reminds me of the deep blue sea when I go on holiday.
Blue reminds me of peaceful birds flying high above me.
Blue reminds me of raindrops falling softly on my back.
Blue reminds me of joyful music when I go to parties.
Blue reminds me of the sky when I look above me.
Blue reminds me of blueberries growing in my garden.
Blue reminds me of my school uniform that I wear.
Blue reminds me of the saint's wheel, the symbol of my school.
Blue reminds me of water coming out of my kitchen tap.
Blue reminds me of happiness when I see a smile.

Niamh O'Dea (8)
St Catherine's RC Primary School, Barnet

Red

Red reminds me of Red Nose Day.
Red reminds me of a ladybird.
Red reminds me of roses standing in the garden.
Red reminds me of Valentine's Day when people love one another.
Red reminds me of God who gave me blood.
Red reminds me of the red tables in my classroom.
Red reminds me of a pencil pot full of red pencils.
Red reminds me of my homework at school.

Gemma Anderson (8)
St Catherine's RC Primary School, Barnet

Red

Red reminds me of Manchester United winning every match.
Red reminds me of the postbox every time I pass it.
Red reminds me of roses smelling beautiful.
Red reminds me of embarrassment when someone embarrasses me.
Red reminds me of Arsenal winning every single match in the league.
Red reminds me of every love heart.
Red reminds me of Santa coming down our chimney.
Red reminds me of the Devil who I don't believe in.
Red reminds me of Valentine's Day when I go to it in my school.
Red reminds me of the red tables in my classroom.
Red reminds me of a pencil pot full of red pencils.

Theodore Soussoudis (8)
St Catherine's RC Primary School, Barnet

Yellow

Yellow reminds me of juicy melons on Christmas Day.
Yellow reminds me of dry bananas in a fruit bowl.
Yellow reminds me of chewy pasta in my mouth.
Yellow reminds me of the shiny sun shining on the beach.
Yellow reminds me of sweet sweetcorn with tuna and pasta.
Yellow reminds me of the holes in yummy Swiss cheese.
Yellow reminds me of butter on the bread of my sandwiches.
Yellow reminds me of the funny smell of lemons.
Yellow reminds me of the big, massive lion in the jungle.
Yellow reminds me of the bright little buttercups in the grass.
Yellow reminds me of the broken up rocks in the sand.

Joseph Davies (8)
St Catherine's RC Primary School, Barnet

Blue

Blue reminds me of the deep blue sea that flows.
Blue reminds me of the water that we drink every day.
Blue reminds me of the sky where birds fly.
Blue reminds me of the bluebirds that sing a little song.
Blue reminds me of the blueberries that people like to eat.
Blue reminds me of the waves that splash onto the beach.
Blue reminds me of the colour blue that we use every day.
Blue reminds me of the raindrops that twinkle in the air.
Blue reminds my teacher of Tottenham Hotspur that win
every match!
Blue reminds me of St Catherine's wheel which St Catherine
broke for Jesus.
Blue reminds me of peace and calm that people like to have.
Blue reminds me of music, especially Blue, you know, the band!
Blue reminds me of my uniform that I wear to school every day.
Blue doesn't remind me of much more,
Not anything more.

Georgina Ennis (8)
St Catherine's RC Primary School, Barnet

Yellow

Yellow reminds me of the daffodils on the grass.
Yellow reminds me of the mango which is sweet to eat.
Yellow reminds me of yellow pencils and books in class.
Yellow reminds me of the sun which gives us light.
Yellow reminds me of the yellow sand on the beach called
Dona Paulaol.
Yellow reminds me of yellow cheese which I love to eat.
Yellow reminds me of yellow balls that are very bouncy.
Yellow reminds me of yellow jumpers that are warm.

Stalin Lincoln De Monte Furtado (8)
St Catherine's RC Primary School, Barnet

Into A Dream

The sun is gleaming,
You are glowing,
Hear the songs,
That birds are singing.
Watch the sunset,
Let the day go,
Follow the love,
That will always grow.
Fall into the night,
A peaceful dream,
Let your eyes close,
Fall asleep.

Danielle Bates (10)
St Catherine's RC Primary School, Barnet

The Sun

I make the sky a clear blue,
Then I add the white, fluffy clouds.
I make the sun set in the sky,
Making the world catch your eye,
With yellow, pink and orange.
Now I make the sky turn dark,
Now I tell my friend the moon,
To just shine on you,
To make the dark seem
Ever so light.

Aoife Hanley (10)
St Catherine's RC Primary School, Barnet

Sunflower

Pop the seed into the ground,
It doesn't make a sound.
The roots slowly shoot out,
Then the stem pops up and looks about
And says, 'I like it here.'
As it grows,
Leaves start to show.
The petals start to settle in different colours,
Then the bees come and treat it like a pillow.
It is fully grown.
As it bends,
It sadly dies,
But that's not the end.

Toni Trevena-Jones (10)
St Catherine's RC Primary School, Barnet

Phil And Lil

Phil and Lil
Went up the hill,
To buy some apple juice.
On the way back
They tripped over a sack.
In the rack,
They had a goose,
The sky was dark,
They went in to have a juice.

Dan Dao (9)
St Catherine's RC Primary School, Barnet

When Someone Dies

When someone dies,
You should not be upset,
You should not feel alone,
For they are always with you.
They shall then say to you,
'I am always looking over you
and protecting.
I have gone to live in a better place,
So don't feel alone,
Don't cry,
For I am always with you.'
When someone dies,
You should not be upset,
You should be happy for them.

Charisse Williams (11)
St Catherine's RC Primary School, Barnet

The Meadow

We all love the meadow
It's quiet and calm
It's bursting with colour
The birds always sing
We all love the meadow.

Amy Bliss (10)
St Catherine's RC Primary School, Barnet

Bill And Ben

Bill and Ben, the flower pot men
They're always so happy, but you don't see them
Hiding in the flowerpot, up the tree
You can try your hardest, but you won't see me!
We're hiding over here, we're hiding over there,
We're hiding in the shed

Uh-oh, here comes the farmer
I hope he's got some wheat only calmer
It's so exciting to have smoked salmon
Oh boy, here come the sparrows
They'll eat it with a few mallows
Along with some more live salmon!

Aaron Li (10)
St Catherine's RC Primary School, Barnet

Snow

Children like
To use snow
For making things
Like snowmen
And have snow fights
And lots more
Snow gives a breeze
And rustles all the trees
And that makes snow fun!

Adam Fathers (10)
St Catherine's RC Primary School, Barnet

Do You Remember Me?

Do you remember me
Who you used to kick and use
Like a punch bag?
You acted like a bully to me.
Do you remember me
Who you called names
And stole money from?
But now I am big and strong.
You can't hurt me
Because I'm strong
And better than you
And I am going to tell you
What you did to me
And see if it hurts *you!*

Rebecca Byrne (11)
St Catherine's RC Primary School, Barnet

My Meadow

Soft colours, green grass,
As far as my meadow goes.
Butterflies come and go
In my little meadow.

Flowers and vines spreading, spreading,
Bumblebees buzz, collecting pollen,
A bench under a shady tree,
A quiet place for you and me!

Jenny McKeen (10)
St Catherine's RC Primary School, Barnet

My Little Sister

My little sister,
Acts like a mister
And loves going on dates.
She kicks your head
And jumps on your bed
And beats up all your mates.

She drinks the rain
And can't feel pain.
My mum said, 'That girl's bad.'
She's very lazy
And very crazy,
I honestly think she's mad.

She escaped from prison
And stole Father Pete's chrism,
Then beat up Muhammed Ali.
She robbed a bank,
Because Titanic sank,
But her smile makes me happy.

Chukwuma Duru (10)
St Catherine's RC Primary School, Barnet

Hamlet

H orrible things are sleeping in the orchards
A snake did not kill me
M urder to get revenge
L et revenge be sweet
E lsinore castle has a traitor
T he snake is sitting on the throne.

Daniel Giraldo (10)
St Catherine's RC Primary School, Barnet

Shakespeare

S pooky noises outside the castle
H orrible nights for the soldiers
A ll the people asleep in the castle except for Hamlet
K illing is going on in the castle
E lsinore castle is getting spooked
S ilent soldiers wait for another visit from the ghost
P olonius' death was a complete accident
E ight people died in the play
A ll of them got murdered
R emember the ghost's words
'E lsinore castle is in danger.'

Casey Norrie (10)
St Catherine's RC Primary School, Barnet

Seasons

Summer brings the sun out,
Everyone goes on holiday.

Winter brings central heating,
Everyone stays indoors.

Autumn brings breezes,
Leaves turn to different colours.

Spring brings new life,
The weather does anything.

Charlotte Foster (10)
St Catherine's RC Primary School, Barnet

The Victorian School

I hate my school!
The day seems so long
Before the teacher puts the chalk
To the board, I gulp.

Homework is another thing
It cries out to me in the night
Heaps of it
That weigh me down.

I'm sure my school's Victorian
Teachers go on about the old days
I dream of a calculator
And freedom!

But when we are dismissed
A window opens
The sun shines
And the school day is over.

George Winterbourne (10)
St Catherine's RC Primary School, Barnet

Hamlet

H amlet had gone mad in the castle of Elsonore
A ll was not well in the castle of madness
M y heart beats too hard when I hear Hamlet
L umber through Hamlet's world and you will be so scared
that you could drop dead
E verything is a horrible mystery of death
T here is so much murder, it's horribly distressing.

Anthony Ward (10)
St Catherine's RC Primary School, Barnet

Missing Angels

When an angel is missing, God sends out a search party.
They tiptoe around when everyone is sleeping
And they sing a special song that whistles down the wind.
If there is no answer, God comes down to Earth.
He checks everything is OK and he looks everywhere.
The birds twitter mystically in the trees,
But don't say a word to one another
And the missing angel puts her finger to her lips
And whispers, 'Pray don't tell.'
She goes to lots of houses and hides inside people,
So that when they wake up and go out into the big, bad world,
They grant wishes and bring peace to everyone.
If the person likes the angel, they thank God secretly
And they drift around telling all the angels' secrets
And making dreams come true.
When the person goes up to Heaven,
Everyone is sad,
But the person replaces the angel
And swims around in a wandering daze.
As the missing angel slips around corners, into people's souls,
Like slipping into a coat, but more magical,
Ready to turn lives upside down.

Elizabeth Thomas (11)
St Catherine's RC Primary School, Barnet

The Ocean

The ocean is a magical place,
Where dolphins swim all day.
The water sparkles like twinkling stars
And shows the sharks the way.

The beautiful sand at the bottom,
Yellow and orange like a fire,
Lets starfish lie in peace
And they will never tire.

There are so many oceans,
The Atlantic, the Pacific and more.
The boats and ferries cut the top,
But it still lies strong at the core.

So now you see what a wonderful place,
Oceans really are.
All the animals are wonderful things,
All special like the stars.

Jennifer Kilby (11)
St Catherine's RC Primary School, Barnet

A Little Speck Of Light

The sky I look upon each day,
Has suddenly become a darkened grey.
The reeds are no longer reaching my knees,
But instead, down in the ground,
Among the seeds.
The pond has gone an icy cold
And the ducks are no longer looking
Handsome and bold.
None of this is stopping me from reaching the end,
I see a tulip which is much alive and my friend.
I raise it into the air
And the sun comes out and shines everywhere.
All the world is colourful again,
Until the next time, when I reach a new friend.

Ivana Scatola (10)
St Catherine's RC Primary School, Barnet

Once Upon A Rhyme

Once upon a rhyme,
There was a robin on a tree.
He said, 'How are you?'
To another robin he could see.
They talked and talked all day,
Then one began to say,
'Will you marry me? I love you so.'
The other said, 'Yes!' and then, 'Ho, ho!'
And they flew off happily.

Once upon a rhyme,
It happens all the time.
Two birds fall in love,
But sometimes a dove,
Oh, once upon a rhyme.

Once upon a rhyme,
The bell began to chime,
1, 2, 3, 4,
A knock on the door.
I wonder who it could be?
An angel from what they can see.
Oh no, it's a man,
With some sort of pan.
He wants a dime,
They give one this time.

Once upon a rhyme,
It happens all the time.
The bell starts to chime,
They give someone a dime,
Oh, once upon a rhyme.

Jennifer Marshall (11)
St Catherine's RC Primary School, Barnet

Wishes

I wish there was no gravity
So I could fly and fly
I also wish there was no truth
So I could lie and lie.

I wish there was no rain
So there would be only sun
I also wish there was a free baker
So I could have a bun.

I wish there were no schools
So I could play and play
I also wish there was no night
So there would be only day.

I hope those wishes do come true
I doubt that they will
I was so busy daydreaming
I forgot my grandad's pill.

Liam Snow (11)
St Catherine's RC Primary School, Barnet

The Night Sky

As the sun goes down behind the hill,
The stars seem to glow
And the sky seems to fill.
The moon appears from behind the misty clouds,
When suddenly the crows fly by
In their crowds and crowds.

As the sky darkens second by second,
The owl twitters and he never gets frightened.
The moon gives a twinkle for all the girls and boys
And the stars play together with all their many toys.
'Soon the dark will go and back will come the light,'
The children tell their parents as they all say goodnight!

Lucinda Rix (11)
St Catherine's RC Primary School, Barnet

The Lesson

Some lessons are boring,
Some lessons are fun.
First the science experiment,
Blowing up in your face
And Flubber being invented,
Bouncing everywhere.

Now it's time for maths,
On a rainy day,
Your dreams of sunny times,
Just floating away.
Now the maths comes,
Out to play,
Chanting our tables,
In a horrible way.

Literacy the most boring,
Of all!
The growling of gremlins,
Say, 'Speech mark, comma,
Full stop, capital letter,'
In my head
And that was my tale
Of the lesson!

Michael Moore (11)
St Catherine's RC Primary School, Barnet

My Dog, Patch!

My dog, Patch,
Is very hard to catch.
He'll hide in my bed,
Also in the garden shed,
Because he's my dog, Patch.

He'll hide under the kitchen table,
Even in a donkey's stable!
Why can't you be like other dogs?
Have a bath or have a wash?
Because he's my dog, Patch.

When it's time to go to bed,
I always look for Patch, my dog,
Then I rest my sleepy head,
After I hear a scratch, jump
And a rough tongue on my face, *Patch!*

Emily Holmes (10)
St Catherine's RC Primary School, Barnet

Today's Forecast

When the sun rises, you can't hear a whisper
Until it reaches nine and the farmers start their duties.
When it gets to noon, you smell the bacon frying.
When the day moves on, you hear the children playing in the field.
Then you hear the mother's voice calling them for dinner.
You hear the family discussing things around the dinner table.
When the day reaches six, you hear the music start to play.
When it gets to 9pm, you hear the children moan and groan as they go to bed.
Then you hear the wine bottles open for the parents to enjoy.
When it reaches midnight, you can't hear a whisper because the town has gone to sleep.

Caitlin O'Kane (10)
St Catherine's RC Primary School, Barnet

Under My Bed

Under my bed,
Is an old packet of crisps,
Gone all mouldy and green,
Along with a couple of my music discs,
An album of a band named Mean Teen.

Under my bed,
My teddy bear said,
'I'm cold, I'm tired, I'm under your bed!'
'I'm sorry,' I say, 'but I've no time for you, Ned.'
'And don't forget me, your pencil with no lead!'

Under my bed,
Is my soft blankie.
People say it's disgusting.
'It's not,' I reply, 'how can you say it's manky?'
There's also a key that's started rusting!

It really is sad to let go,
But Mum's going to check my bed.
So they have to be gone for tomorrow,
So goodbye Ned!

Lauren Nickolls (10)
St Catherine's RC Primary School, Barnet

A Valentine Poem

V alentine's Day is a special day
A ll the boys and girls get together
L ove is a powerful thing
E veryone has a special person they like
N o one has got a friend they don't like
T ogether, girls and boys will be kind
I n their hearts they truly love each other
N ever ever will they tell them, but surprise them if they can
E njoy their company please
S t Valentine made this day, so be brave and put your
troubles away.

Ria Rowland (10)
St Catherine's RC Primary School, Barnet

My Pet Rat, Jimmy

My pet rat, Jimmy,
Lives under the floor.
My dead cat, Kimmy,
Was squashed under the door.

My pet dog, Tim,
Lives on top of the cat.
My pet horse, Jim, eats out of the bin
And is sick all over the house.

My pet chameleon, Liam,
I can't even see 'im.
My pet fly, Sam,
Only eats ham with a bit of jam.

And after that I was banned
From any animal for life,
Until I went to the zoo.

Lewis Maidment (11)
St Catherine's RC Primary School, Barnet

Valentine's Day

V iolets are given to those who are loved.
A ll the boys are with the girls.
L et the boys give you a rose.
E njoy this day and go somewhere nice.
N ever be nervous, just be nice and brave.
T his day will only come once, so make the most of it.
I magine you're a princess.
N ever let go of your valentine.
E ven if he's trying to dump you, don't let go.

D iscos are open, so why not go.
A lways be nice on this Valentine's Day.
Y ou're the one for me, forever.

Kathryn McKenzie (11)
St Catherine's RC Primary School, Barnet

What If?

One day a little old man gave a boy 26 reasons
Not to go to school?
He said . . .
What if you get beaten up?
What if you get told off?
What if you miss your playtime?
What if you start to cry?
What if you get sick and die?
What if you fall over?
What if you have to go to the headmaster's office?
What if it starts to rain?
What if you get sunburnt?
What if you don't get taller?
What if you get smaller?
What if your hair doesn't grow?
What if you grow green hairs on your chest?
What if you get your spellings wrong?
What if you get an X on your work?
What if the buses aren't running?
What if a football hits you in the face?
What if you start to choke?
What if they close the swimming pool?
What if there's no water?
What if the football bursts?
What if it snows?
What if there are gunshots?
What if the teachers don't come in?
What if it's too hot?
What if you get kicked?
That is why you should not go to school.
The boy went home crying.

Daniel Subandrio (11)
St Catherine's RC Primary School, Barnet

As I Gaze

As I gaze upon
The glistening water,
I see blues,
I see purples
And I see mauve.

As I gaze upon
The sunset,
I see pinks,
I see reds,
And I see yellows.

As I gaze upon
All these things,
I am really gazing
On the face of God,
Who looms in everything.

Teresa Nunziata (11)
St Catherine's RC Primary School, Barnet

The Talking Trash Can

I am the poor trash can
who gets to eat the slimy toothpick,
I want to be sick!
They're taking the mick.
Then every Monday the dreadful moment comes,
The trash man.
He lifts me upside down,
It feels like my brain has gone into the garbage truck.

One day the baby emptied his potty in me,
Then Wilber put his snotty tissue in me!
Next Monday when the trash man came,
Instead of emptying me,
They put me in the trash truck.
Now *I'm* trash.

Miles Lenehan (11)
St Catherine's RC Primary School, Barnet

Teacher's Pet

As the dreary school bell rings,
You know that no bird will sing at school.
For you see there is no place on Earth,
That could possibly be worse
Than school.

You will understand that
Since the beginning of time,
Man and boy alike
Have hated
School.

As Shakespeare said,
'And then the whining schoolboy with his satchel
And shining morning face.
Creeping like a snail
Unwillingly to school'.

But unfortunately,
There is somebody
Who likes the dreary,
Very weary
School.

But who?
I hear you wonder.
Well, there's no need to ponder
On such a silly question,
For the answer is quite simple.
It is a . . .
Teacher's pet!

Calum McAfee (11)
St Catherine's RC Primary School, Barnet

Seasons!

There are four reasons,
Why you should be glad in all four seasons.
Spring is brand new and pretty,
Cuter than a brand new ginger kitty.

Summer is hot with lots of fun,
Because the sun is shining on.
We all go in our swimming pool,
Then we get out and we're nice and cool.

Autumn is when everything's dying,
All the people just keep on sighing.
Leaves are falling to the ground,
But they don't make any sound.

Winter is when everything's white
And you can't see anything in sight.
All the trees are really bare,
But no one actually really cares.

So in conclusion,
There are my seasons
And my very interesting reasons.

Natalie Quilter (11)
St Catherine's RC Primary School, Barnet

My Day

There was a football match one day,
But my mum said I couldn't play.
I pleaded with my coach,
He said, 'You're the best,
Take a rest.'

At the end of school,
I went in the pool,
As I was so hot,
I heard someone shout, 'Good shot!'

When I got home,
I started to moan
That I'd left my homework at school,
My sister started laughing like a mule!

When I went in on Monday,
Of hope there wasn't a ray.
I got a detention,
That I shouldn't have mentioned,
So that has made my day!

James Isaac (10)
St Catherine's RC Primary School, Barnet

The Good And The Bad

The people from the heavens,
Sit above the clouds,
The men who come from horrid Hell,
Sit below our feet.
The butterflies are in the skies,
While rats are crawling on the ground.
Those who are up above are free,
But their enemies are slaves.
God is kind and fair,
Satan's wicked, wicked, wicked.
While one is only wanting fairness,
The other just wants power.
The air in some places is nice and fresh,
But some is smoky.
There is one place of love
And always somewhere of hate.
The good side has a worship place,
But the bad side doesn't bother.
Someone died for the good,
But no one died for the bad.
In case you didn't notice, God must be the good one,
While Satan is the worst.

Sam Steele (10)
St Catherine's RC Primary School, Barnet

The Red Balloon

Red balloon at the party,
Bouncing up and down,
Floating out the window
And all around the town.

Kundai Nyazema (7)
St Michael's Woolmer Green Primary School, Woolmer Green

Colour Poem

Red is for Valentine's Day,
Red is for hearts,
Red is in the rainbow,
Red is in wine.
Your tongue is red,
Red is in our counting stick,
Red is in Mars,
Blood is red.
A rose is red in summer,
Manchester United wear it on their shirts.
Fire is very dangerous, that's why it's red.
Sunset has stripes of red in it that looks very pretty.

Emily Wintle (7)
St Michael's Woolmer Green Primary School, Woolmer Green

Purple

Purple is for pansies,
Beautiful as blossom.
Purple is a queen's robe,
It's purple at the bottom.
Purple on a pencil case,
A purple crayon to trace.
You wear a purple party dress
And feel very special.

Victoria Swain (7)
St Michael's Woolmer Green Primary School, Woolmer Green

The Purple Poem

A purple balloon sparkles like glass.
A purple ring glimmers in the sunlight.
A purple tiara shines like a ring.
A purple necklace sparkles in the moonlight.

Laura Tomlinson (8)
St Michael's Woolmer Green Primary School, Woolmer Green

What Is Blue?

A sapphire shines like water trickling down a stream.
A blue, velvet box full of treasures, beautiful they seem.
Tears fill children's blue, shining eyes
As they trickle down their cheeks,
Just like a tap with water trickling down.
All different blues, light ones, bright ones,
Navy, turquoise, dark.
A dolphin rolling in the waves, as smooth as silk.

Emily Orna-Ornstein (7)
St Michael's Woolmer Green Primary School, Woolmer Green

All I See Is Black

Oil, armour, they're all black.
Dark clouds, rotten teeth, they're black too.
The dark clouds are as black as Man United's away shirt.

I look around and what do I see?
Headphones, black ink,
Computer screen and Class Two's radio.

All I see is black.

George Taylor (8)
St Michael's Woolmer Green Primary School, Woolmer Green

Red

Red balloons as high as a red devil,
Floating through the sky.
One by one they pop and fall,
On to passers-by.
Red paint dripping on the floor,
Slowly running under the door.

Lawrence Goddard (9)
St Michael's Woolmer Green Primary School, Woolmer Green

When I Grow Up

When I grow up
I hope that I'm a football player
For West Ham.
When I grow up
I hope that there will be hover boards
And talking cars with no wheels.
When I grow up
I hope that there will be good weather
Everywhere.

Sebastian Byrne (9)
St Michael's Woolmer Green Primary School, Woolmer Green

When I Grow Up

When I grow up
I wish to be a football star
And play for the best team.
I wish to be with the best players
And win all the cups,
To win the league,
Then we will win
And be called the champions.

Kamal Samsudeen (8)
St Michael's Woolmer Green Primary School, Woolmer Green

Springtime In The Future

Trees shaped like ice cream cones,
Leaves shaped like mobile phones.
Flowers that never die,
Never-ending apple pie.
People whizzing as fast as cheetahs,
Cuddly rabbits as personal heaters.
The grass is pink,
The world is made of rainbow ink.

Amanda Mowforth (8)
St Michael's Woolmer Green Primary School, Woolmer Green

When I Grow Up

When I grow up I wish to see,
The moon with intelligent life.
When I grow up I wish to see,
No more guns blasting.
When I grow up I wish to see,
Hoverboards speeding down the track.
When I grow up I wish to see,
Cars with no wheels,
Blasting off at rocket speed.

Christian Sloan (9)
St Michael's Woolmer Green Primary School, Woolmer Green

Blue

A gleaming river like a bright bird.
The crashing, rolling sea like the thundery sky.
I hear all the rain tickling on my heart.
I can hear all these things crashing in my ear.
Then! I saw a glittery sapphire in my eyes.

Molly Davis (7)
St Michael's Woolmer Green Primary School, Woolmer Green

The Blue Day

Clouds in the light sky,
Birds sing,
Butterflies are flying,
Birds eat in a berry bush.

Leanne Jones (7)
St Michael's Woolmer Green Primary School, Woolmer Green

A Merciless Sea

The waves will crash on the rocky shore,
The seagulls fly as the sea will roar.
The fish will fight the fast flowing sea,
Struggling through until they're free,
As free as free can be.

The sea fights mercilessly,
The ferociousness is in this verse,
It swallows boats and bells without dings
And lots of other little things,
What terror could it bring?

But when the sun slowly arises,
The sea has other great surprises,
As children wade through the harmless shallows,
Kids on the pier eating marshmallows
And see the sea of blues and yellows,
Shining on the surface.

Carl Papworth (10)
St Peter's School, Rickmansworth

A Taste Of Autumn

Looking around me I can see,
Leaves twirling and swirling off a tree.
Different colours everywhere,
The wind throws them whistling,
'I don't care!'
Screaming and shouting, I'm having fun,
The joy of autumn has just begun.

Enjoying the leaves and playing around,
I have just realised that I have found . . .
A taste of autumn.

Lauren Burton (10)
St Peter's School, Rickmansworth

Can You Write A Snow Poem?

We awoke to see,
The snow that glistened,
The sound of a robin on snow,
We listened.

It fell so fine
And laid on the ground,
Flakes still falling,
Twirling, twisting round and round.

Like a sheet of white,
Falling everywhere,
It fell so softly,
Gently with care.

I watched the snowflakes,
Lying snow on snow,
The sunlit brightness,
The dazzling glow.

Beautiful now,
But later on,
It will turn to slush,
The whiteness and brightness . . . gone!

Olivia Kiernan (10)
St Peter's School, Rickmansworth

The Snow

I can't wait to get in my white blanket,
Having snowball fights till seven.
Waking up the next morning with slush.
My dream has melted away.

Zahra Aboobaker (10)
St Peter's School, Rickmansworth

Inspiration

Colours in a painting,
The right patience in waiting,
Rewinding throughout my life.

Spilling juice when I was younger,
Wailing with hunger,
Inspiration is the key to all of these things.

Growing up already,
Walking straight and steady,
Inspiration is there,
There throughout your life.

Nicola Jones (10)
St Peter's School, Rickmansworth

Rubbish

Remember that old Coke can that you left on the park bench?
Remember the old Tesco bag that you let blow away?
Remember those old sweet wrappers that you left littering a trail on the street?

A small squirrel got its head stuck in your Coke can.
A rabbit was suffocated in your Tesco bag.
A sparrow choked on one of your sweet wrappers.

Think before you litter.

Joelle Fitch (10)
Sheering CE Primary School

Seasons

Winter's child,
Winter's weather,
Makes ice and snow go wild,
Then spring breaks open its cocoon
And releases weather quite mild,
But spring is not as powerful,
As the blazing summer heat
And summer vanquishes spring,
In what is a heartbeat,
Then autumn leaves cover up the blazing summer sun
And create coloured confetti,
Which some say is quite fun.

Rachael Krishna (10)
Sunny Bank Primary School

What Is The Snow?

The snow is cloud
landed on Earth.
It is a white, silk sheet
spread over the land.
It is a thousand bits of confetti
falling from the sky.
It is a white T-shirt
just out of the wash.
It is a giant, white shoebox
flattened for recycling.

Katie Silvester (10)
Takeley CP School

What Is The Moon?

It is a fifty pence piece
Dropped into a sewer.
It is a white dot
On black paper.
It is a bullet hole
In a black door.
It is a bit of chalk
In fresh tarmac.
It is a big chunk of rock
On a road.

Ciaran O'Donohue (10)
Takeley CP School

What Is The Moon?

The moon is a spot of white paint on a black dust sheet.
It is a feather floating from the sky.
It is a tiny white mouse curled up in a black hole.
It is a white balloon floating into the night sky.
It is a piece of fluff on a black, silk sheet.
Or a speck of dust on a black carpet.

Sophie Hickles (10)
Takeley CP School

What Is Rain?

Rain is a giant's shower turned on full blast.
It is a cloud crying out with sadness.
It is a huge tap being turned on maximum.
It is a lot of small buttons, showering the world.
It is dragons' drool dripping over the world.
It is giants' blood spilling from a huge gash.

James Westlake-Jones (10)
Takeley CP School

What Is The Wind?

God breathing down on you,
A shadow running past you,
A propeller spinning around in your face,
A giant doing a whoops-a-daisy,
God sneezing across the town,
A giant's girlfriend blow-drying her hair.

Edward Beanland (10)
Takeley CP School

The Moon

The moon is a round candle lit up at night
A giant lump of cheese dropped by a giant
It is a dustprint of a finger on black paper
It is Jesus' football on God's greenhouse
A mouldy orange dropped from God's tree.

Adam Claydon (10)
Takeley CP School

What Is A Star?

A star is a silver sequin on a stretched piece of black paper.
It's a 5p coin chucked into the moonlit sky.
It's a silver bauble in a dark, old mansion.
It's a silver earring dropped into a pot of ink.
It's a light bulb flickering in the darkness of a house.

Thomas Brown (9)
Takeley CP School

What Is The Sea?

It is a giant's bath with a yellow towel on the side,
A giant puddle waiting to be splashed in,
An uncovered world waiting to be discovered,
An angry creature when he feels like throwing a storm,
A scuba-diver's attraction to different types of fish,
It is a blue blob on a piece of paper glittering in the sun.

Brittany Malcolm (9)
Takeley CP School

What Is The Moon?

The moon is a giant tennis ball hit high into the sky.
It is a face that grew so big it could not fit on the Earth.
It is a giant scoop of ice cream flicked high into the black night sky.
It is the biggest splodge of mashed potato splashed into space.

Zach Field (9)
Takeley CP School

What Is The Snow?

Cotton wool cloud that floats slowly down,
Glitter sprinkled across the world,
A giant's dandruff drifting across the field,
A white duvet covering the world.

Stephanie Duke (10)
Takeley CP School

My Dares

My dare is
To drink Fairy Liquid,
To swallow a spider,
To munch a light bulb,
Now remember, this is just a reminder

My dare is
To post a pin,
To represent a heater,
To lick the ground in Trent park,
To find a metre

My dare is
To eat my socks,
To use the boys' loo,
To introduce my thumb,
To wear a false arm!

Sue Shaker (9)
Trent CE Primary School

My Name Is . . .

My name is turkey sandwich
My name is blue
My name is football eyes
My name is goo.

My name is chicken bits
My name is Mr Geezer
My name is dog
My name is Mr Wheezer

My name is bouncy balls
My name is motorbikes
My name is kitten
My name is going on hikes.

Max Heale (8)
Trent CE Primary School

Nervous

I felt nervous when I fell over,
My hands were shaking like an earthquake,
I felt nervous when I got told off in class,
My knees were knocking like a blizzard.

I felt nervous when it was the Christmas play,
My head was thumping vigorously,
I felt nervous when I broke a school ruler,
My tummy felt like butterflies were fluttering inside it.

I felt nervous when I broke up with my friend,
My arms felt like a herd of elephants trampling on them,
I felt nervous when I had a doctor's appointment,
My legs felt like somebody was hitting them.

Betty Moody & Lucy Hall (9)
Trent CE Primary School

My Name Is . . .

My name is sports fiasco
My name is chocolate fudge cake
My name is watching motor racing
My name is make and break

My name is play on the computer
My name is building robots
My name is go on holiday
My name is tying knots

My name is swing on chair
My name is jumbo jet
My name is slam a door
My name is bite a finger pet.

Murray Knott (8)
Trent CE Primary School

My Name Is . . .

My name is David Beckham
My name is Michael Owen
My name is Ronaldo
My name is write a poem

My name is Mr Chinese
My name is Mr Bacon
My name is toffee apple
My name is Mr Mistaken

My name is ruler
My name is pencil
My name is sharpener
My name is stencil.

Will Smith (8)
Trent CE Primary School

My Name Is . . .

My name is Miss McChicken
My name is Despina
My name is special
My name is drink lots of Ribena.

My name is Miss Pencil Case
My name is agony and pain
My name is salt and vinegar crisps
My name is the driver of a train.

My name is candyfloss
My name is Miss Christmas Cake
My name is rubber girl
My name is Miss Chocolate Shake.

Despina Markou (9)
Trent CE Primary School

The Old House

The rain pounds at the window
The wind screams to be let in
A creeper slowly and silently climbs the walls
Looking to the silence within.

The curtains are made of silky spider's lace
And the stairs groan with misery
He once knew a time of splendour
And wealth for all to see.

Lightning strikes a tree
And makes a yellow flame fly high
The cold house has not felt heat
Since it was left here to die.

The flames creep up to the house
And are slowly let inside
They devour and eat all they see
There is no place to hide.

The flames reach up into the night
Say hello to the stars and the sky
The house screams its last goodbye
And slowly, silently dies.

Rose Michael (11)
Trent CE Primary School

Space Soot

Solidly, protecting, helmet
Glass, protecting, frame
Fastly, creepy, glove
Slowly, breathing, oxygen panel
USA, moving, arm
Electric, moving, control panel
Fat, floating, leg
Foot, flying, shoe.

Luca Cioffi (8)
Trent CE Primary School

My Name Is . . .

My name is flute puffer
My name is crispy chips
My name is wibbly jelly
My name is red, sweet lips

My name is Miss Crazy Art
My name is Simpson mad
My name is Monopoly fun
My name is making boys sad

My name is Captain Chocolate
My name is climbing trees
My name is pedal fast girl
My name is grubby knees

My name is legs panting
My name is music tune
My name is chocolate roll
My name is see you soon.

Beth Pendock (8)
Trent CE Primary School

My Name Is . . .

My name is spotty dog
My name is Miss Chocolate Cake
My name is rubber pencil
My name is fruit cake

My name is Miss Numbers
My name is doggy waggy
My name is flippy fish
My name is doggy froggy

My name is Master Chocolate
My name is Mr Blue
My name is bike rider
My name is Mrs Flue.

Millicent Alexander (8)
Trent CE Primary School

Ode To A Hamster

Hail hamster, my furry friend,
I adore you in every way possible,
You are my best friend and no one elses,
You smell so fresh and clean,
You make me happy when you are near me,
I love you and envy you in every way possible,
I appreciate the way your arms stick out for a cuddle,
You are my number one, my only number one.
I wrap you around myself on cold, wintry nights,
If I lost you I would find you, I promise I would.
Your ginger colour is wonderful,
You are my ginger-flavoured hot chocolate,
You are my little teddy bear,
You are a hamster, no, a golden hamster,
The sweetest hamster on Earth,
I could taste you from here,
You are my hamster
And my only
Ginger hot chocolate.

Naomi Hunt (11)
Trent CE Primary School

An Ode To My Watch

Oh watch, indescribable watch.
The picture of flames in the centre of your beautiful face makes my heart race.
The orange second hand ticks slowly, which sounds like a scratching noise.
When I press the tiny pin into the side of your wonderful grey bottom, your face lights up turquoise.
The Velcro strap with *Timex* printed on and fraying elastic dazzles me, especially when I see the zigzags on it.
The oval shaped rim round your face I adore,
You are my watch, my special watch.

Oliver Clixby (10)
Trent CE Primary School

Ode To A Teddy

Hail to the wondrous, smartest teddy.
How cool and so cuddly you can be.
There is no one better and more enchanting than you.
You may be chubby, but you are more adorable than anything
in the world.
You smell so fabulous and fresh that anyone could eat you.
You are definitely eye-catching and comforting.
You feel smoother than anything.
You are obviously my number one!
You mean everything to me.
You sleep with me every night to make me happy.
I can smell you every day in my bed.
You are my best friend and I envy you.
I'd do anything in the world just for you.
You are the best and I love you very much!
I praise you every day and you always bring me good luck!
I am very proud of you and I wrap my arms around you so tightly!
You are my sugar plum and also my superstar.
You are sensational!

Ibrahim Yildiz (10)
Trent CE Primary School

My Name Is . . .

My name is I drink Fanta
My name is hide in logs
My name is Master Pasta
My name is walk the dog

My name is King Pancake
My name is stay up late
My name is horseback
My name is fish bait

My name is chimpanzee
My name is Master Toffee
My name is washing machine
My name is don't like coffee.

James Reavell (9)
Trent CE Primary School

My Name Is . . .

My name is smelly sock
My name is super Sam
My name is French fries
My name is delicious lamb

My name is maths homework
My name is the winner
My name is a big house
My name is Mister Sinner

My name is pencil case
My name is manky rat
My name is reading book
My name is cute cat

My name is black rubber
My name is dictionary
My name is sharp scissors
My name is burglar Barry.

Samuel Langley (8)
Trent CE Primary School

My Name Is . . .

My name is Master Saxophone
My name is fast chopper
My name is eating sweets
My name is slow hopper

My name is Mr Pizza
My name is Captain Lock
My name is Dr Attic
My name is hating frocks

My name is mucky shirts
My name is stained wheat
My name is rusty hot
My name is creating heat.

Cem Yildiz (9)
Trent CE Primary School

Ode To My Ornament

Oh, beautiful ornament.
How I treasure your beauty with all my heart.
You smile every time you see light, which gives me shivers
down my spine.
You are stunning with your amazing powers.
Your sleek, smooth, shiny effect on your skin makes me smile
with delight.
I feel joyful when I hear the sea through you.
How graceful the brightness of your skin shimmering is.
If I am upset you bring happiness to me.
Your thrilling colours are spectacular.
You are so mighty, with clay so strong.
I admire your carefully made parts.
You are exquisite.
You remind me deeply of the sea.
You are an ornament.
My ornament.

Emily Matthews (10)
Trent CE Primary School

My Ode To Busted

Oh, my unique Busted
How I worship your talent in singing and admire your lyrics
Your clothes are the best make
You are so precious to me
You have a gift to rock my world
You are my treasure
My one of a kind
I will never buy another CD with the name 'Pink' on it because you
are my idol, my number one
My special band Busted, I worship you
You are my only prize possession
Oh, when I met you my heart raced so fast
I could have won a race
You are mine.

Demi Constantinou (10)
Trent CE Primary School

Ode To The Flux Deluxe Pencil Case

O' hail to the Flux Deluxe pencil case!
I adore your cuddly texture.
When I am blue you make me ecstatic.
I worship your spaceman logo as you float around
Your starry galaxy.
I love your cute, little spaceman face!
I cherish you.
I adore you.
I love you.
I love your black, sparkly outfit!
I love your blue writing!
I like the way you can hold all my pens and pencils.
Oh, you are the best pencil case.
You're not just any pencil case.
You're my pencil case.

Kara Herty (10)
Trent CE Primary School

Ode To My Teddy, Cola

Oh, irresistible Teddy Cola,
How I worship your enchanting hard, rough nose,
I adore your velvety warmth and your gazing eyes.
When I feel lonely, I gently hoist you into my arms
And I feel the pieces of my broken heart
fixed back together once more.
Your eyes are identical to twinkling stars
and when I stare into them, I feel valued.
When you popped out of that birthday wrapping paper
I knew we would be friends forever.
You are delightful,
You are irresistible,
You are ravishing,
You are superb,
You are exquisite,
You are the foremost supreme teddy - Cola.

Georgia Trupia (10)
Trent CE Primary School

Ode To A Teddy Bear

O' wondrous teddy bear
How your furry texture sends a shiver down my spine.
You are my saviour. I enjoy your constant cute look.
I praise your beautiful fluffy skin.
You are my treasure and my love.
Your soft, snowy coat makes me feel delighted and grateful
that I have you.
I wouldn't reject you for the world.
Your smell is like a beautiful red rose.
I love your colourful top saying 'I love you'.
It makes me feel so blissful.
When I wake up, I see your adorable face looking at me.
I will never touch another teddy again.
I will never talk about or cuddle another teddy again.
You are my favourite teddy and I will never do anything bad to you.
You are my teddy bear.

Georgia Symeou (10)
Trent CE Primary School

Ode To A Pokémon Annual

O' hail, almighty Pokémon Annual,
I love your smooth and hard cover.
You look so detailed.
I praise your texture and your brilliant, blazing colour.
I adore your pictures.
I treasure you like a million pieces of gold.
I love the way you shine in the light,
The way you make the Pokémon look.
You are wondrous, you are dazzling.
I wish you would never change as long as I live.
I love the way you give me endless stories about Pokémon.
I cherish you and I will never let anybody else have you.
You are a book.
My book.

Joshua Ugboma-Battams (10)
Trent CE Primary School

Ode To My Football Boots

Reign O' football boots
Your colour is like the moon on a clear night or the silvery
scales of a fish
Your distinctive Adidas symbol stands out over the blood-red tongue
Your beautiful, cosy inside comforts my feet
Your three elegant stripes look like a tiger has scratched you,
but your incredible body has healed it.
You kick the ball like it's a balloon and your swift swing hits it
with such speed and accuracy
When I take you out of my bag, I feel like a different person,
a better person
When I step on the pitch, everyone looks at you, jealous of
your fashionable look
You smell of that delightful fragrance - mud
I adore the way you are put together
Your puffy coating protects me from injury
Thank you football boots
My football boots.

Robin Pendock (10)
Trent CE Primary School

My Pokemon Annual

O my Pokemon annual book,
I adore your pretty pictures
And worship the feel of your pages on my fingers.
You are my favourite annual.
I love how you pull me into true happiness.
I cherish your bright colours
And the way your pages sway
And make the sound *ssssssss* in the wind.
You are the perfect book for me.
I like the way your pages tickle my chin.
Oh, the things you have in store for me
When I open you up.
Oh! My Pokemon annual.

Stefan Philip (10)
Trent CE Primary School

Ode To A Book

O' wondrous entertainer, O' elite bringer of joy,
You are as precious as a diamond.
I admire your sleek and slender look and that glint in your cover,
I'm immersed in your beauty and splendour.
You smell like fresh, new clothes just opened from a pack,
Light and airy, yet strikingly brilliant.
The smooth feel of your pages puts a baby's bottom to shame.
When I flick through, I can hear a soft tapping noise,
Which is better than any band's music.
Oh, how I wish I could taste you,
But then you'd be tarnished and be wearing a cloak of shame
Because of my dirty drool.
You catch everyone's eyes with your cover that's as beautiful
As a rainbow.
Alex Rider super spy, you're the best.
O' book, you a re everything to me
And much, much more.

Rahul Rajakulasingam (10)
Trent CE Primary School

Ode To My GameBoy SP

You provide unconditional light with the push of one button
You shine with cleanliness, beautiful and new
You are a 32-bit, platinum coloured goddess
Your sensors are perfect
Your buttons are immaculate
You smell of new
You use an expensive lithium charger
I stare at you and the world stands still
When I saw you, I knew that my life was complete
I envy your smooth platinum cover
No one can compare with you
All other objects bow to you
Someone could offer me £150,000 and I would say *no!*
Because you are mine and mine alone.

Dami Ajuwon (10)
Trent CE Primary School

Ode To A Pair Of Football Boots

O' exquisite football boots, you bring joy and
happiness to my life.
As I run through the grass with you, you cut through
the mud so sleek and slender.
I adore your strong and hard structure.
When you hit a ball, it goes flying.
I love it when I play with you.
We are a great team and I have such an enjoyable
time with you.
I worship you in every way, you stand out from every other.
I praise you.
You are brilliant and beautiful.
Without you I would be lost.
You are my prized possession, my lifeline.
I admire your red tongue and Adidas sign,
it stands out from the rest.
O' football boots, others envy me because I have you.
You are my football boots.

John Maycock (11)
Trent CE Primary School

Spring

Spring is when the birds fly
Up in the sky
Over the baby lambs.

Chicks sing sweetly
As daffodils sway in the
Early morning breeze.

The sun is shining
As the blossoms' colours
Brighten up the day.

A new life is born
As the world wakes up
From its long winter sleep.

Charlotte Michael (8)
Trent CE Primary School

Ode To A Flute

Hail, O my fabulous flute, I wish I could hold you forever.
When I first get you out of your exquisite velvet case,
My hands tremble as I fasten together your cold structure.
I honour your ability to produce a sound as clear as crystal
With no effort at all.
I cherish the way your smooth, silver keys change the note,
With absolutely no concentration.
O! How I worship your ability to play jazzy tunes in classical ways.
I will never look at another lute,
Never play another piano,
Never touch another trombone,
Never clasp another clarinet,
Never set eyes on another saxophone.
You are the only one for me.
Your silver twinkles like the stars in the sky.
I shiver when I take apart your head, spine and tail.
Surely the gods of the Greek myths sent you to my arms.
You are divine, you are one of a kind.
You are a solid piece of metal.
My flute.

Emma Bird (10)
Trent CE Primary School

Man On The Moon!

Helmet hard protecting head.
Mask transparent reflecting.
Gloves warm soft.
Backpack safe hard.
Logo shiny glimmering.
Oxygen control panel.
Trousers smooth slippery.
Boot hard protecting feet.

William Hayes (8)
Trent CE Primary School

Ode To A Photo Album

O' wondrous photo album, a praiseworthy book of memories.
Touching your smooth, glossy cover excites me.
I adore all the names on your back,
Reminding me of sweet past that jumps out at me in bright colours.
You smell of brand new pages, so fresh!
O'! Your beauty rises above all others,
Your bright clothing puts others to shame.
You are cold and refreshing to touch,
But when I open you, you fill me with warmth.
Nothing more could I want of you, for you are above the best.
I revel in the way you crinkle as I turn your perfect pages.
I cherish the quiet bang as I close you.
Yes, you are the most perfect object on Earth.
Your bold, bright colours,
Your smooth, shiny texture,
Your slightly squashy cover!
Beautiful photo album, you are the best.
You are a prized photo album,
My photo album!

Grace Pereira (10)
Trent CE Primary School

My Name Is . . .

My name is Miss Teacher
My name is Bakewell Tart
My name is Miss Cheeky
My name is Little Miss Smart

My name is chewing pasta
My name is best friend Millie
My name is dolphin lover
My name is worst friend Tilly

My name is chocolate ice cream
My name is beautiful blonde
My name is little line up 4
My name is Miss Fond.

Sarah Bailey (8)
Trent CE Primary School

Ode To A Teddy

Hail, oh precious teddy,
How I admire you,
I treasure you as the greatest toy in the world!
You're the only toy for me.
You are extremely lovable to me,
You look the most glamorous teddy ever and always will be!
I love the way you smell like a brand new toy every single day.
How I adore you in every way.
I think you are brilliant!
You're the cuddliest toy and so very cute.
I think you're absolutely the best!
I worship you in every way,
I take you everywhere with me,
I hear you say how happy you are with me.
Every day I honour you as superbly as I can.
You are my King and always will be.
You are everything to me.
I could not survive without you!
I appreciate you do as much as you can for me.
You are only mine and will always be mine.
Oh teddy, you give me sheer delight.
You are a teddy.
My teddy!

Amelie Zambon (11)
Trent CE Primary School

My Homemade Hamster

Hail to the chocolate hamster
I praise your floppy, minute ears
I gaze in wonder at your wide-eyed stare
I adore your chocolate, fur-covered coat
I love your gliding, swishing tail
I treasure you above finest jewels, above the greatest gold
I would not trade anything for you
You never butt in or talk above me, you never bite
I praise you to the heavens for that
At night you are my fierce guardian,
You are my jewel, worthy of the highest king
I worship you for your obedience, never fighting, never biting,
You have never had a bad thought or an evil idea
And for that I worship you
You send shivers down my spine when I stroke you
I dance for joy when I see your loose ends
By day you are my greatest friend and companion
By night you are my protector
When I wake up, you beam and say good morning
At night you tuck me in
You are my hamster
My hamster, my homemade hamster.

Edward Robinson (11)
Trent CE Primary School

Ode To My Model

O' elegant model
How divine you are when I put you together
When I feel your sleek, cut parts
I marvel in wonder at the warmth I see within you
When I smell your sensitive smell, I sniff in wonder
Your neat compactness sends me jumping for joy
I cherish you O' Nessie of the deep
My senses are excited by you
With your teeth you can hold anything for me
As you sit in your lake you look so gorgeous
I just want to pick you up and cuddle you
I embrace you O' Nessie, Master Nessie, Mr Nessie, Sir Nessie
You are my hopes and dreams rolled into one
As I turn on your motor, the push button clicks and fills me with envy
As I take you down the park, people offer me a million pounds for you
But I say *no!*
You are more to me than that, not even a billion pounds
Could persuade me to part with you
Your eyes are like emeralds in a pile of coal
I will never part with you
You are my star in the night, my sun in the day
You are, my model.

Calum Knott (11)
Trent CE Primary School

Ode To Mr Dog

O' Mr Dog, my cuddly dog teddy,
How I cherish your stubby legs and spongy centre,
I love the way you lose your cotton wool stuffing all over the house,
I love the way you have to be repaired all the time!
    Never will I touch a teddy bear,
    Never will I feel a feline,
    Never will I stroke a snake,
    Never will I pat a panda,
    Never will I hug a horse,
And Mister Dog, never will I feel a fish,
Mr Dog, I will never leave you!
I admire the old smell of you and I treasure your orange
                        tikka masala tarnish!
    You are the best,
    You are incomparable. You are Mr Dog!

Mark Taylor (11)
Trent CE Primary School

Ode To A Hairbrush

O' precious hairbrush, how I adore you when you run through my hair.
I remember how you became mine.
When a fabulous friend and I parted, you were placed into my hands.
I cherish the way your chipped parts remind me of how old you are.
I could never bear to look at another hairbrush, not even if it had
                the same Mulan design on its back as you.
I treasure the way I feel your black spikes rub against my hand.
I adore the way your red, sparkly glitter shines out above the rest
                        of my hair accessories.
I cherish the soft noise you make when I pull back your spikes.
I adore the way you never complain if you find a knot in my hair.
You are the most precious item I have.
If I lost you, I would not sleep, eat or drink until you were back in
                                my hands.
O' treasured hairbrush, how I love you!

Shekira Khan (11)
Trent CE Primary School

Ode To My Watch

O' incredible watch, how I adore the way you keep me cheerful,
I admire your hushed, repetitive tick-tock, tick-tock,
Your rich, shining gold brings you glorious colour,
Your stunning leather is a comfort to me as I sleep, eat,
drink and do many other exciting things with you,
I envy your clear, black numbers as I remember,
You were given to me by my granny and granda,
As you touched my hands, all those years ago,
happiness spread through my body,
I am amazed by your unique style and your identical six holes,
You always tell me the exact time as you are so reliable,
I love you even though you have been repaired once,
You are my protector,
I couldn't bear to part with you ever,
It would be like losing my best friend,
I would cry and cry until you were found,
You are my watch, my only watch.

Kate Hendry (11)
Trent CE Primary School

My Name Is . . .

My name is Miss Drink Lots Of Coke
My name is hide-and-seek
My name is Captain Cake
My name is hide and then peek.

My name is eating pizza
My name is Queen Crumble
My name is stay up late
My name is my tummy rumble.

My name is Master Michael
My name is monkey
My name is watch TV
My name is Mrs Funky.

Martha Ratcliff (8)
Trent CE Primary School

Ode To A Book

Hail book, full of wonderful words and eye-catching pictures.
How could I live without you?
You are everything to me. You are a perfect size.
Small enough to carry around and put in my pocket.
Filled to the brim with interesting facts and handy stories.
You never complain.
I want to read your story forever.
I take you everywhere with me.
You are my idol, my number one.
I could not go anywhere without you.
You are the grandest, most special object in the world.
You outstrip teddy bears, yo-yos and all those rubbish toys.
You are divine.
You are beautiful.
I worship all your stories and thank you.
Oh book, you give me sheer delight.
Your knowledge is outstanding.
I am proud to be with you.

Amelia Hunt (11)
Trent CE Primary School

Ode To Monkeys

O' wondrous monkeys, I adore your cheeky looks
I praise your constant smiles
I like the way you hang on my cupboard doors
I love you so much that I will never look at another teddy again
You look so new, you are always gleaming, which makes me delighted
You are my marvellous teddies
I treasure you with all my heart
I like the way you swing your tails and curl them up
Your brown, soft skin comforts me at night when it is cold
I admire your hard eyes that shine like the sun
You are my special monkeys.

Dimitri Christofi (11)
Trent CE Primary School

Ode To Kimberly Bear

O' wonderful teddy,
Your soft fur means everything to me,
You send shivers down my spine when I look into your
big, brown eyes.
Your feet are so soft that I want to hold you upside down
but it would hurt your feelings.
Your brown Bear Factory label tells me where you were born
and where you came from.
Your blue, sewn in, limited edition label is brilliant and beautiful,
it makes me want to stare at it day after day.
I adore your white, soft, cute and cuddly coat.
Your brown nose makes me tremble with ecstasy.
I savour you as I cuddle you close at night,
knowing I'm going to have to leave you as I go to school.
What I would do without you, I would never know.
Your fluffy, white tail I adore and wish I could have one for myself.
Your tea-stained right elbow is unique.
My heart starts thudding like horses' hooves when I look at you.
You can walk where you want, whenever you want.
You are a bear, my Kimberly Bear!

Joanna Delaney (10)
Trent CE Primary School

Condor Ferry

Whoosh, whoosh, through the sea,
Bang, bang, on the waves,
Grind, grind, the engines go,
This is too heavy for me to carry.
Slurp, slurp, go the drinks,
I don't feel so happy now,
I hate the smell of diesel all the time,
So I'm going to be sick, I know!

George Bateman (10)
Watton-at-Stone Primary & Nursery School

Questions, Questions, Stop Asking So Many Questions!

Mum, where are we going?
We're going to Frimley.
Why?
To meet your uncle.
Are we there yet?
No. Hopefull we'll get there in about an hour.
An hour! What am I going to do for an hour?
Play I Spy.
What if I don't want to play I Spy?
Well don't play it then.
Are we there yet?
You've already asked me that.
OK then, can I have my packet of crisps?
Oh . . . go on then.
What do I do when I've run out of crisps?
Throw it in the bin. Wait, pass it to me.
Mum, will I starve? Will I die?
No. You won't starve and you won't die.
Can you predict the future then?
Yes.
Can you teach me?
No.
Are we there yet?
Hey, are you listening to me?
No!
Stressy!
Are we there yet?
Yes!
Hooray! Sis, why are you dribbling?
Don't start.
Mum, tell Annabel to shut up!
Shut up!

Annabel Lee (10)
Watton-at-Stone Primary & Nursery School

Mums, Mums

Mums, mums, always washing,
They're always dashing
And always bashing.
They want to get more cash,
They always have potato that is mash
And mums are always poshed up
And they are mainly grumpy.
They do more cooking than playing games,
Need more time to get more cash,
But too much bashing around in the car
And mums are crashing in the car,
They have a munch before their lunch.

Micah Allen (8)
Watton-at-Stone Primary & Nursery School

When I Need The Toilet

'Are we nearly there yet?'
'No, just stop asking.'
'But I need the toilet.'
'Well try and hold on.'
'I can't, please let me go.'
'I would if I could, but there isn't a toilet for a long way.'
'Can't I just go out of the window or something?'
'No, just stop and shut up.'
'Ohhhh!'
'What now?'
'I think I just wet myself.'
'Well I can't do anything until we get there anyway.'

Thomas Monk (11)
Watton-at-Stone Primary & Nursery School

Question And Answer Poem

Mum?
What?
Can I have a motorbike?
No.
Can I have a petrol scooter then?
I said no.
OK Mum.
Mum, can I have a dog?
No.
What can I have then?
Nothing.
Can I have some sweets?
No, no, no.
Well, can I have a fish?
OK then.
Can I have a carp or a frog?
No, you're not having a carp and a frog is not a fish. You can have
a goldfish.

I don't want one now.

Shane Clay (11)
Watton-at-Stone Primary & Nursery School

The Hot, Sunny Day

A hot, sunny day is coming to an end
Like an ice cream melting into its cone
Whilst the sun is going down
Like a light switch getting switched off.

The hippo was in the water
Like a lily on the pond
The butterfly flew gracefully over the hilltops
Like a gentle breeze
The snake slithered in the grass
Like a slow-moving stream
The puppy in its kennel
Like a cuddly teddy bear.

Katie Simpson (10)
Watton-at-Stone Primary & Nursery School

Where Are We Going?

'Where are we going?'
'You will find out when we get there.'
'Just tell us.'
'I said you'll find out when we get there.'
'Are we nearly there yet then?'
'We will tell you when we are there.'
'Go a bit faster then, but I don't see why we couldn't stay
at the beach.'
'Is this it, a petrol station?'
'No, we are still not there.'
'Hurry up then.'
'Five minutes, then we will be there.'
'OK!'
'Finally, we've got here. Is this it? *Excellent!* Glad we didn't
stay at the beach!'

Emma McAllister (11)
Watton-at-Stone Primary & Nursery School

The Cold And Warm

The rats are very cold,
Like the snowy mountain
And the owl is very old,
Like water in the fountain.

The snail's warm in its shell,
Like heatwaves from a fire
And the crabs ride in the heated bell,
Like hobbits in the shire.

The snake hides in the grass,
Like spiders on their web.
It's slithering very fast
And its tail is glowing red.

Kyle Wilkie (11)
Watton-at-Stone Primary & Nursery School

Diving In The Sea

I'm going diving today,
I wonder what I'll see,
I'm going diving,
I wonder what there'll be.

Look at the fish swimming by,
Their colours of blue and green,
They shimmer from the light above,
The loveliest fish I've ever seen.

I like all the coral,
It's lovely and pink,
Oh no, an octopus,
He's spraying his ink!

It's time to go home,
My air's running low,
Goodbye pretty fish,
I really must go.

Hannah Cooke (9)
Watton-at-Stone Primary & Nursery School

Hamster

I'm a hamster, look at me go,
I'm not slow, so look at me go.
Running round the house at night,
Scurrying back in fright.
It's that cat, that mangy cat,
Sitting on the baseball bat.
Then there came a mighty fright,
When the cat tried to bite.
Suddenly my owner came,
Then the cat got the blame.

Matthew Wilkinson (9)
Watton-at-Stone Primary & Nursery School

Oh Mum

'Mum, what are you talking about?'
'Nothing, go and sit down.'
'Can I watch TV?'
'Yes, if it will get you out of here.'
'Oh Mum, can I have this game? It's so cool.'
'No, you can't.'
'Why?'
'Cause we can't afford it right now.'
'Oh poop. Can I have this game then?'
'No you can't.'
'Meanie.'
'I heard that.'
She hears everything.

Stephen Sperring (11)
Watton-at-Stone Primary & Nursery School

Light Can Be . . .

Light can be a light bulb in a room
Light can be a bomb going *boom*
Light can be a lion in the savannah grass
Light can be gold found in a narrow pass.

Light can be the sun high above
Light can be a yellow dove
Light can be a firework going *bang*
Light can be a yellow gang.

James Hankin (10)
Watton-at-Stone Primary & Nursery School

My Two Cats

My two cats
Run around at night,
Up and down the stairs
Having a fight.

Ozzy and Moto
Crazy they are,
Climbing up the curtains
Not getting far.

Now it's bedtime
They close their eyes,
And start sleeping
Like little cutey pies.

Jake Rochford (9)
Watton-at-Stone Primary & Nursery School

I'm A Little Football

I am a little football
I once was brand new
I am covered in dark patches
And my colour's navy blue.

Although I am so small
I can bounce really tall
I can go high in the sky
And watch the birds fly.

Mitchell Allen (9)
Watton-at-Stone Primary & Nursery School

Football

Do you like football?
I think it's great.
It's the best game in the world,
Because you can play it with your mate.

Do you like football?
I think it's cool.
Two teams playing each other,
To see who can get the ball.

Do you like football?
I think it's wicked.
Everyone tries to score,
But it hurts when you are kicked.

Do you like football?
I think it's brill.
Score lots of goals,
To give the crowd a thrill.

Do you like football?
I think it's good.
Do you play football?
If not, I think you should.

Michael Searle (9)
Watton-at-Stone Primary & Nursery School

Mars

One day as I lay in the park
Looking at the stars,
I wondered how much fun it would be
To go up to Mars.
So I opened my bag
And ate my Mars.
Oh no! There are so many cars,
I will just have to fly myself
Home to Mars.

Lewis Stewart (9)
Watton-at-Stone Primary & Nursery School

Animal Poems

My name is Bobby
And I am a cat
I crossed the road
And suddenly went *splat.*

My name is Freddy
And I am a dog
I fell in the pond
And swallowed a frog.

My name is Ronnie
And I am a rat
I live with my nan
And her name is Pat.

My name is Toby
And I am a monkey
I go to school
And my friends think I'm funky!

James Hall (10)
Watton-at-Stone Primary & Nursery School

My Poem

Once there was a little bat
That got eaten by the rat.
The rat got eaten by the mat
And the mat got eaten by the cat.
The cat got hit by a bat
And that was the end of the dumb old cat.

Joe Dix (10)
Watton-at-Stone Primary & Nursery School

My Cat

My cat just eats and sleeps,
He's always lying on my bed in a heap.
He never goes outside or he'll get his fur wet,
Sometimes I wish he was never ever my pet.
When he goes outside, his paws are muddy,
He goes on my bed, so when I go in it's not so cuddly.

My cat has silky, ginger fur,
This silky, ginger mog goes *purrr.*
But whenever he's not asleep or munching,
He sticks out a paw and starts punching.

To keep himself warm he sits above the fire,
But on one occasion his tail caught fire.
Even though he's somewhat dim,
No matter what, I'll always love him.

Alexandra Smith (10)
Watton-at-Stone Primary & Nursery School

My Special Friend

My special friend I love to see,
I hope she feels the same as me.
We love to play and have lots of fun,
Especially when we chase and run.
We like to have a song and dance
And don't give our other friends a chance.
She always makes me laugh a lot,
I realise what a great friend I've got.

Shannon Aylott (9)
Watton-at-Stone Primary & Nursery School

My Garden

In my garden every day
I see things that make me say
Hip hip hip - hip hip hooray
Things are wonderful today.

Mrs Blackbird sings her song
While noisy magpies chat along
Deep red roses stand and pose
Bluebells bob and touch their toes.

Baby birds call from their nest
To mother tit in her blue vest
Fluttering butterfly and buzzing bee
Are welcomed gladly to find their tea

Mr Spider's web I spy
Hanging down to catch a fly
Wind blows foxgloves to and fro
Then wind chimes ring to tell us, go.

Rain is coming and we must flee
Birds all shelter in the tree
Insects hide in flower beds
Blossoms bend their cheery heads.

My garden is a lovely place
Which makes a smile come to my face
It is the place I love to be
And all of this I get for free.

Jessica Lo Monaco (9)
Watton-at-Stone Primary & Nursery School

The Alien From Mars

There was an alien from Mars
Who stole a lot of cars
He thought it was cool
But looked like a fool
And now he's been put behind bars.

Liam Reynolds (10)
Watton-at-Stone Primary & Nursery School

My Scary Pet Shop

This is a funny poem
About my scary pet shop.
If you don't like freaky things
I think you'd better stop.

In my scary pet shop
We have rats that eat the bats
And lizards that suck human blood,
That gobble up our cats.

In my gruesome pet shop
We have snakes with rattling cages
And bright, bright red chinchillas,
Who sleep on the Yellow Pages.

In my calamity pet shop
We have dogs that look very ghastly
And blue and turquoise crocodiles,
That smell of muddy parsley.

In my extraordinary pet shop
We have fleas and nits and gnats,
A Komodo dragon has just been born
And it does minute cowpats.

In my scary pet shop
We have (as you might have known),
A lot of strange things happening,
Which in writing I have just shown.

Nicola Bramley (9)
Watton-at-Stone Primary & Nursery School

Nonsense Poem

I walked to school in my car,
We did English at midnight whilst eating our lunch.
The next day we went to B&Q and did DT,
Then we went home in the car and had dinner on my bike.

Jordan Parfitt (10)
Watton-at-Stone Primary & Nursery School

Very Old Clock

I am a very old clock
I like to tick and tock
The other clocks say
'You've had your day'
But still I tick and tock.

I am a very old clock
I like to tick and tock
I have a grand key
That will only fit me
It makes me tick and tock.

I am a very old clock
I like to tick and tock
New clocks have batteries
That come from factories
And I still tick and tock.

I am a very old clock
I like to tick and tock
Some clocks have power
That might last an hour
But I still tick and tock.

I am a very old clock
I like to tick and tock
I am 100 years young
And have never been resprung
And I still tick and tock.

I am a very old clock
I like to tick and tock
Sometimes I chime
To keep me on time
That's because I'm a clock!

Ashley Hawker (10)
Watton-at-Stone Primary & Nursery School

Chocolate Poem

Different types of chocolate
Have different types of taste,
I don't know why people do what they do
By going and putting it to waste.

I eat my Creme Eggs two at a time
I save my Crunchies for Friday,
I agree that a Mars helps you work, rest and play
But I only wish I had one every day.

It tastes so exquisite, it tastes so delightful
When I'm down, it raises my mood,
My life would not be worth living
If I had any other type of food.

George Pattle (10)
Watton-at-Stone Primary & Nursery School

School Work

M onday morning, what have we got?
A ddition,
T ables,
H orrible hexagrams and heptagons are next,
S ubtracting all my knowledge.

L earning is really tiring, here's what we've got,
I dioms,
T enses,
E xclamation marks,
R eference books,
A bbreviations,
C ommas,
Y es, we're finished for today.

Grant Robins (10)
Watton-at-Stone Primary & Nursery School

Siskin The School Cat

Siskin sits on my lap,
Siskin makes the children flap,
Because she herself is the schooling cat
Who wipes her paws on the doormat!
The children chase her round and round,
The children pet her on the ground.

Tabitha Walton Lane (8)
Watton-at-Stone Primary & Nursery School

The Song Of The Cotton Wool Cats

Cotton wool cats are asleep at night,
Cotton wool cats are awake when light,
Cotton wool cats are brave and can fight,
They beat up other cats with all their might.
Cotton wool cats change their pitch when they itch,
Mostly people call them tiny titch.

Sophie Simpson (8)
Watton-at-Stone Primary & Nursery School

Super sized Cats

Super sized cats are fierce and bite,
Super sized cats are very tall,
Super sized cats go out at night,
They like to chase mice down the spooky hall.

Super sized cats love to bite,
Super sized cats like to fight in the scary night,
Super sized cats hop over the wall,
They bang their heads and crush their paws.

Chloe Moncur-Byrne (7)
Watton-at-Stone Primary & Nursery School

Song Of The Boffin Brain Cat

Boffin brain cat is clever and bright,
He sticks up his nose because he's always right.
Boffin brain behaves very well,
Got a long tail, trips over it well.
Boffin brain cat, little body and huge head,
He is a brainbox, never in bed.

Boffin brain cat gets freezing cold,
Never ever uses mould,
Gets in a pickle, sorts himself out,
Every day has a bit of trout.

Helena Brown (8)
Watton-at-Stone Primary & Nursery School

The Song Of The Gardener Cats

Gardener cats are soft and grey
Gardener cats are around in May
Gardens and shovels
In the day they bite
Tidy gardens after midnight
And loads of gasps at dawn
When people look at their lawn.

Sophie Bell (8)
Watton-at-Stone Primary & Nursery School

The Song Of The Sickable Cats

Sickable cats are black and white,
Sickable cats only come out at night,
They even take over the light and night.

The sickable cats are bad,
Sickable cats are cool,
Sickable cats are bad,
Sickable cats are lazy bones.

Jack Bateman (7)
Watton-at-Stone Primary & Nursery School

The Brainless Cats

Brainless cats are black and white
Brainless cats come out tonight
Brainless cats are lovely
Brainless cats are rather big.

Brainless cats cannot catch mice
Brainless cats are scared of rabbits
They make them jump up trees.
Brainless cats are bright and light
Brainless cats have silly hats.

Callum Ball (7)
Watton-at-Stone Primary & Nursery School

The Cotton Wool Cats

Cotton wool cats are creamy white,
Cotton wool cats can fight and bite,
Cotton wool cats are large and tall,
Cotton wool cats swim in pools.

Cotton wool cats run after bikes,
Cotton wool cats are very cool,
Cotton wool cats go night hiking,
Cotton wool cats score goals.

Ryan Buxton (8)
Watton-at-Stone Primary & Nursery School

The Song Of The Sumo Cats

The sumo cats are sly and strong,
The sumo cats are kings of all and never wrong.
They rule the night and are never fooled,
Sumo cats are black and white.

Liam Welch (7)
Watton-at-Stone Primary & Nursery School

The Miracle Cats

The miracle cats are silver and gold,
The miracle cats play with a ball,
The miracle cats are never sold
And like to swim in the open pool.
The miracle cats are always happy,
The miracle cats are never sad,
The miracle cats like a person called Patty.

Christopher Toumbas (7)
Watton-at-Stone Primary & Nursery School

Cotton Wool Cats

Cotton wool cats are furry and white,
Cotton wool cats are mainly boys,
Cotton wool cats are clever and bright,
Look at them play with their favourite toys.
Cotton wool cats have sad, strange faces,
Cotton wool cats have bright blue eyes.

Annabel Tabone (7)
Watton-at-Stone Primary & Nursery School

Snowy Cat

The snowy cat is cold,
The snowy cat goes outside,
The snowy cat is very bold,
But snowy cat goes astride,
The snowy cat finds some gold,
But snowy cat doesn't mind.

Jessica Owen (7)
Watton-at-Stone Primary & Nursery School

Greedy Cat

Greedy cat
Is a moody cat
And he often says hello to Postman Pat,
He really likes a pat.

Greedy cat has very small legs,
Greedy cat has a rather small head,
Greedy cat tries to eat all Mum's pegs,
He is a very naughty cat when he goes to bed.

Greedy cat is big and round,
When I go to get a snack,
In the kitchen that's where he's normally found,
Sometimes it's in my lunch pack.

Charlotte Dix (8)
Watton-at-Stone Primary & Nursery School

Horrible Cats

Horrible cats come out tonight
Horrible cats are black and white
Horrible cats are very bright
Horrible cats are mean and selfish
Horrible cats are rather huge
Horrible cats are really dumb
Horrible cats have furry, white tails.

Dannielle Knott (8)
Watton-at-Stone Primary & Nursery School

Fluffy Cat

Fluffy cat is a hungry one,
And is very fat.
His favourite snack is a bun.
This fluffy cat is cool,
Fluffy cat has small legs,
Fluffy cat has a paddling pool.
Fluffy cat sometimes begs.

Eleanor Hardcastle (8)
Watton-at-Stone Primary & Nursery School

The Cuddable Cat

The cuddable cat is fluffy and white,
The cuddable cat is tiny and small,
The cuddable cat purrs all night,
The cuddable cat likes to play with a ball,
The cuddable cat does not bite,
The cuddable cat is not very tall.

Lucy Jenkins (7)
Watton-at-Stone Primary & Nursery School

Super size Cats

Super size cats are fierce and they bite,
Super size cats are very large,
Super size cats go out at night,
They like to chase mice down the hall.

Harry Mack (7)
Watton-at-Stone Primary & Nursery School

Cakes

Cakes, cakes are so yummy,
If you don't like them, you're a dummy.
Cakes, cakes smell so good,
Even better than a Christmas pud.
Cakes, cakes look so great,
I might give one to my best mate.
Cakes, cakes are fun to make,
Why don't you try, go on have a bake.
'OK,' my sister said,
But soon we have got to go to bed.

Cakes, cakes I hear them crying,
Or maybe they're just lying.
Cakes, cakes shall I see,
If they're just lying to me?
Cakes, cakes are they OK?
If they are they will have to pay.

I need to know, shall I have a bite?
No one will know, it's not light.
OK, OK, it's lying,
'I've caught you red-handed eating my cakes.'
'Sorry, maybe tomorrow we can have another bake!'

Paige Oakley (9)
Watton-at-Stone Primary & Nursery School

Cotton Wool Cats

Cotton wool cats come out at night,
Cotton wool cats are cool and small,
Cotton wool cats are very bright
And pleasant to hear when they are called.
Cotton wool cats are rather cool,
Cotton wool cats always play pool,
Cotton wool cats are always sleeping in the pool,
They like to practise their leaping around
And they like to wake in the morning light.

Finlay Everington (7)
Watton-at-Stone Primary & Nursery School

My Toys

My toys are definitely not boys,
When I'm asleep they might move,
You know what, they might do a groove!
I have quite a few,
But they're not that new!
They're really soft,
Even the ones in the loft.
When I'm not there they might play,
What do you think, hey?
I go to bed with my ted!
I wake up in the morning
And they look a bit boring.
I go downstairs for a drink,
My brother gives me a wink!
I had a bit of toast,
Then I heard the post.
I went to do my hair,
I thought I saw a stare.
I like my toys,
Whether or not they're boys!

Olivia Salvage (9)
Watton-at-Stone Primary & Nursery School

Fuzzable Cats

Fuzzable cats are really fun,
My fuzzable cat is a sleepy cat,
My fuzzable cat likes to be in the sun,
The fuzzable cat is a dreamy cat,
The fuzzable cat is a sly cat,
The fuzzable cat is a bit bossy,
Fuzzable cats like eating pie,
Fuzzable cats are a bit snotty.

Alexandra Cunningham (7)
Watton-at-Stone Primary & Nursery School

The Horrible Victorian

A wooden chair,
A horrible dare,
A gorgeous dress,
A big mess.
The whole world is looking at me,
I saw them all just staring at me.
What I did was really bad,
I hurt that innocent lad.
I am the horrible Victorian,
The secret I hide is another story,
You would hate it because it is gory.
I hate myself for what I've done,
So I'd better run and run.
Don't let me tell the story,
Or you will end up like that lad, Rory.

Sophie Manarin (9)
Watton-at-Stone Primary & Nursery School

Chocolate

Chocolate, sweets are so yum,
So is Hubba-Bubba gum.
The ones that are nice is every one,
If you don't like them, then you're dumb.

Crisps are nice, biscuits too,
They even sell them at the zoo!
They sell them in all sorts of sizes,
The shapes give you a lot of surprises!

When you don't have any in the house,
Urgent! Urgent!
Catch the mouse!

Chloe Kiln (9)
Watton-at-Stone Primary & Nursery School

Nature

Nature, nature, nature,
Sticks and branches in the woods,
Dirt and soil on the ground,
Where the worms are out of bounds.
Living creatures in the cold,
They are hibernating from the ghastly cold.
Trees are blowing fast,
One has fallen down from a gale.
Green leaves on the ground,
There are thousands on the ground,
Blowing everywhere.
Grass is green
And animals and creatures
Live there very alone.
Nature, nature, nature.

Cameron Landels (9)
Watton-at-Stone Primary & Nursery School

Watching TV

I was watching TV
With my dinner on my knee
There was a giant pea
And I ate it slice by slice
With a chainsaw.
My mum grilled a pizza
And I scoffed it all up.

Joe Fryers (8)
Watton-at-Stone Primary & Nursery School

Fireworks

Fireworks are fun, fireworks are great,
Some fireworks go over my garden gate.
Some fireworks shoot up in the sky,
Some can even fly.
Some fireworks spin
And some land in the bin.
Some fireworks are fast,
Some fireworks are slow,
Some even put on a show.
Catherine wheels spin really fast,
Some even come flying past.
Rockets shoot up in the sky,
Which makes little babies cry.

Megan Vosper (8)
Watton-at-Stone Primary & Nursery School

Fuzzable Cats

The fuzzable cats are silver and gold,
The fuzzable cats are very cool,
The fuzzable cats eat all the mould,
They like to swim in the swimming pool.

Jacob Coggin (8)
Watton-at-Stone Primary & Nursery School

Cotton Wool Cats

Cotton wool cats are black and grey,
Cotton wool cats are tall and long,
Cotton wool cats are bright and smelly
And pleasant to hear when they run along.
Cotton wool cats have very shy faces.

Callum Armitage (8)
Watton-at-Stone Primary & Nursery School

I love Chocolate

I love chocolate and lovely sweets,
So do most people who I meet.
Lovely, lovely chocolate bar,
Shiny wrapper like a star.
Caramel chocolate is the best,
It is better than all the rest.
Lollipops are delicious,
I sneak them into my room.
But my mum is suspicious,
I think she'll find out soon.
Maltesers are so light,
I saw one, there was a fight.
I love chocolate, it's so tasty,
I love it so much,
I love sweets so much, much, much.

Harry Jones (9)
Watton-at-Stone Primary & Nursery School

The Hockey Man

There was a boy called Jocky
Who loved to play hockey
He whacked the puck into the goal
And he jumped up and down and said, 'Pow!'
He tried to do it again
But he missed
So he stamped up and down.

Matthew Hartfield (8)
Watton-at-Stone Primary & Nursery School

Sammy The Rabbit

Sammy the rabbit has a bad habit
Of eating lots of food,
Sammy the rabbit is a good mother
Or maybe a spy but undercover.
She likes to be cuddled
But goes back muddled,
She lives in a hutch
She cleans it too much.
She has a mate
That she can sometimes hate.
She bosses him around
He tries to hide but he is always found.
I love my rabbits.

Alex Sapsford (9)
Watton-at-Stone Primary & Nursery School

Fat Cat

I went to the shop and bought a kitten,
She was black and white and I named her Mitten.
She acts like a maniac when she is inside,
When we are in the garden she runs down my slide.
A few months later I opened up my eyes
And looked at her with surprise.
I didn't find her cute now, she was lazy and fat,
She did nothing all day but sit on my lap.
She can't get through the cat flap, so we have to open the door,
Whenever she has her dinner, she will always want more!

Daniele McGrath (8)
Watton-at-Stone Primary & Nursery School

Wacky People

All around the towns,
People dressed in gowns.
Everyone in wacky cars,
That look like they're from Mars.
People in clothing shops,
All buying red and blue tops.
Girls and boys on the train,
On their way to Pudding Lane.
Going along the pathways,
Until they heard a lot of neighs.
Along to the farm to feed the horses,
Time to see Mrs Moorses.
Along to the hairdressers,
Until they see a man selling umbrellas.
Oh no, it's starting to rain,
Now my knees are in pain.
Now it is time to shoot a gun,
Now my poem is finally done.

Louise Brett (8)
Watton-at-Stone Primary & Nursery School

Fireworks

In the darkness of the night,
In the midnight cold,
Did you see the sparkler
As it scattered stars of gold?
Did you see the rocket,
Zoom into the dark sky?
And hear the bonfire burst
As the flames touched the guy?
In the darkness of the night,
In the midnight cold,
Did you see the Catherine wheel,
Raining showers of gold?

Alice Kingslake (8)
Watton-at-Stone Primary & Nursery School

A Day In The Life Of A Pencil

Oh no, it's ten to nine
The kids are waiting in their line
I know I'm a pencil, but I am frightened so . . .
Don't let them pick me up because they will have a good go

When they go out for playtime
Those fifteen minutes are all mine
But when they come running through the door
I really think I'm very poor

When they do literacy
They are very, very unkind to me
All that writing down on paper
I wish I could say I will see you later

As soon as they go out for lunchtime
I call, 'If someone gets me out of here, I'll give 'em a dime'
Sometimes they throw me in the bin
Because they think I'm too old or thin

So there you go, there's the story of me, the pencil
They really hurt me when they use the stencil
Enough of that talk, I'm just trying to get them in trouble
But when I do they squash me like a bubble.

Maria Wilkie (9)
Watton-at-Stone Primary & Nursery School

The Rabbit

There once was a rabbit,
Who had a peculiar habit,
Made shapes out of straw
And sharpened his claws.
What a strange habit,
For a tiny little rabbit.

Claire Hart (9)
Watton-at-Stone Primary & Nursery School